16.95
COPY 1

VGM Opportunities Series

OPPORTUNITIES IN
CHEMISTRY CAREERS

John H. Woodburn, Ph.D.

D0424885

Foreword by
Glenn T. Seaborg
Nobel Laureate in Chemistry
University Professor of Chemistry for
the University of California

VGM Career Horizons
a division of *NTC Publishing Group*
Lincolnwood, Illinois USA

Cover Photo Credits:
Upper left and lower right courtesy of the DuPont Company; upper right and lower left courtesy of the National Cancer Institute.

Library of Congress Cataloging-in-Publication Data

Woodburn, John H.
    Opportunities in chemisry careers / John H. Woodburn.
        p.   cm. — (VGM opportunities series)
    Includes bibliographical references (p.   –   ).
    ISBN 0-8442-4653-0 (alk. paper). — ISBN 0-8442-4654-9 (pbk. :
alk. paper)
    1. Chemistry—Vocational guidance.   I. Title.   II. Series.
QD39.5.W64   1996
540'.23—dc20   96-9350
                                                        CIP

Published by VGM Career Horizons, a division of NTC Publishing Group
4255 West Touhy Avenue
Lincolnwood (Chicago), Illinois 60646-1975, U.S.A.
© 1997 by NTC Publishing Group. All rights reserved.
No part of this book may be reproduced, stored in a retrieval
system, or transmitted in any form or by any means,
electronic, mechanical, photocopying, recording or otherwise,
without the prior permission of NTC Publishing Group.
Manufactured in the United States of America.

6 7 8 9 VP 9 7 6 5 4 3 2 1

CONTENTS

The first stepping-stone: Chemistry is properties. The second stepping-stone: Chemistry is invisible. The third stepping-stone: Chemistry is reshuffling. The fourth stepping-stone: Chemistry is energy. The fifth stepping-stone: Chemistry is unlimited. The sixth stepping-stone: Chemistry is cooperation. The seventh stepping-stone: Chemistry is particles. The eighth stepping-stone: Chemistry is counting. A final step: Chemistry is labs and demos. Troubles along the way. Some specific problems.

A sample opportunity. A second opportunity. Build a place to live and they will come. Every enemy has a weakness. Everything from smelly fish to blue jeans.

Sensitive questions. Making other contacts.
Application letters and resumes.

First, chemistry is worldwide. Second, chemistry is
a way to make a living. Third, chemistry is products.
Fourth, chemistry is process.

The Code of Ethics of the Chemical Institute of
Canada. The American Institute of Chemists Code
of Ethics. The objectives of the American Chemical
Society.

From Shakespeare to the National Institutes of
Health. A glimpse of tomorrow's chemistry.
Chemists can expect controversy. History revisited.
The image of chemistry back a long way. From recipes
to mental models. Where will future markets be?
Focusing on environmental problems. Keeping
humanity well fed.

ABOUT THE AUTHOR

Dr. John H. Woodburn began his career as a high school science teacher. He went on to hold teaching, R&D, and administrative positions at Michigan State University, Illinois State University, The National Science Teachers Association, and The Johns Hopkins University. He has also served as a consultant to the Atomic Energy Commission and the U.S. Office of Education and has maintained an active interest in the career guidance activities of the American Chemical Society. For the final years of his career, he returned to teaching high school chemistry.

Dr. Woodburn has written a number of books for young people. These all reveal his concern for the intellectual and personal capabilities related to the successful pursuit of science. In addition to *Opportunities in Chemistry Careers,* he is the author of *Excursions into Chemistry, The Whole Earth Energy Crisis,* and *Taking Things Apart and Putting Things Together.*

The author holds a bachelor's degree from Marietta College, a master's degree from Ohio State University, and a doctorate from Michigan State University.

ACKNOWLEDGMENTS

The chemistry-related careers of many people make this book possible. Each citation deserves an expression of gratitude. The following people are representative of those whose contributions may or may not be otherwise identified.

Nanette Butterworth, American Chemical Society; David P. Dahle, Morton Automotive Safety Products; John W. Daly, National Institutes of Health; Donald J. Lyman, Lacey, Washington; Colleen Martin, University of Delaware; Everette L. May, Medical College of Virginia; Amel R. Menotti, Bristol-Myers Squibb; Napoleon Monroe, Survival Technology, Inc.; Julianna B. Pax, Montgomery County (Maryland) Public Schools; Gale Thirlwall-Wilbee, Canadian Society for Chemistry; Michael K. Yorke and Todd Clark, Grace Dearborn.

FOREWORD

You think you may be interested in a career in chemistry. This book will be a wonderful tool to help you to understand the many opportunities throughout the world open to chemists. Perhaps it would also be useful if I shared with you some of my thoughts on the value and rewards of a career in chemistry.

I have been a chemist for more than sixty years, but until I entered my junior year in high school, I had no exposure to science and, therefore, little knowledge of its possiblities. Largely due to the enthusiasm displayed by my high school teacher for the subject, chemistry captured my imagination almost immediately. I had the feeling, "Why hasn't someone told me about this before?" From that point forward, I felt I wanted to become a scientist and bent all my efforts in that direction. I have never been sorry, for I have found in science a life of adventure and great personal satisfaction.

We live in a money-oriented society, but I think that personal success in money matters is often overrated. I believe that every person has a deep psychological need to feel that what she or he is doing has importance, aside from the money paid for doing it. Scientists would feel this sense of purpose and inner satisfaction even if their efforts were not important to the world in which we live. In actuality, of course, there is no group of persons on whom society as a whole depends so heavily. Science has exciting challenges to meet. Great discoveries with great benefits to human beings everywhere are much closer than the far horizons, and the technology necessary to utilize these great discoveries for the better health and quality of life of mankind provides an immense field for your efforts. The scientific discoverer is the first to see or to know a really new thing: she or he is the locksmith of the centuries who has finally fashioned a key to open the door to one of nature's secrets. This age of discovery has changed to new frontiers in space, medicine, biology, artificial intelligence, new sources of energy. The possibilities are almost limitless.

You can be part of it.

Glenn T. Seaborg
Nobel Laureate in Chemistry, 1951
University Professor of Chemistry for
the University of California
Associate Director-at-Large of the
Ernest Orlando Lawrence Berkeley
National Laboratory

INTRODUCTION

When you ask people how they find ways to make a living, you get a variety of answers. Some say they take advantage of whatever opportunities come their way. And these people tend to stay with a job only until something better comes along. Eventually they settle down doing whatever enables them to live as best they can. Other people say they take a job or follow a career if it is offered to them in a way they cannot refuse.

Then there are those who make a project out of finding a way to make a living. They mull over why some people are happy with their jobs or careers while others are not. They see that for some people their work provides much of what is needed to enjoy life, while for others, their paychecks are the only satisfactions their work provides, and they must look elsewhere for the things that make life really worthwhile.

This book is for those who believe there are things we can do to improve our chances of making good career decisions. For example, here are some questions you may want to consider if you are thinking about chemistry-related jobs or careers.

Will I like doing what chemists do? Does chemistry offer an opportunity to make my life count for something?

What does it take to cause a person to like being a chemist? There may be a catch here. It isn't easy to like chemistry without first becoming good at doing chemistry. At the same time, rarely can one who doesn't like chemistry become a good chemist. Fortunately, both sets of circumstances can develop simultaneously. But this may call for considerable patience.

Is chemistry for only the very bright? Do chemists need special skills? There are no easy answers here. It is very unlikely that there are chemistry genes in the human genome. At the same time, just as intelligence seems to come in a range of intensity, jobs and careers in chemistry require a range of intellectual abilities. And it is satisfying to know that success in chemistry usually comes with making the most of everything you have going for you and by learning from the successes (and failures) of other people.

Are there special personality requirements? Do chemists need to be able to win friends and influence people? Of course, but so do people who follow other ways to make a living. Chemists do seem to be individualistic when working as members of a team, however.

Will there be chemistry-related jobs waiting for me if I make it all the way up the education and training ladder? The answer here depends upon circumstances chemists cannot control. Job availability is tied in with economic conditions in general. But we do know that there are more than one million people in the United States who are earning their living in chemistry-related jobs and careers. In fact, it is a rare community that doesn't have at least a few job opportunities where it is an advantage to be trained in chemistry.

Do employers discriminate against women, people of color, those who have minority ethnic backgrounds, or the physically handicapped? A definitive answer to these questions could be misleading. It is to be expected that all employers will give all job applicants a fair shake and that there are to be no "glass ceilings" in the way of gaining promotions. At the same time, there are job situations in the chemical enterprise where employees share responsibility for everyone's safety. Under these circumstances, employers are obligated to hire only those people whose physical condition or other personal attributes will enable them to deal successfully with any emergency that may arise. When one is seeking a job, common sense favors emphasizing capabilities and credentials and delaying suspicions of unfair treatment until actually encountering unfair or discriminating treatment.

Will I enjoy working with the kinds of people who choose chemistry-related jobs and careers? This is pretty much up to you, the kind of person you are, your attitudes and values, how you treat and expect to be treated by others. All kinds of people become chemists. In general, however, we expect chemists to be creative and eager to get things done.

But don't chemists sometimes mess up the environment or produce materials that harm people or set civilization back? Yes, chemists risk becoming involved in projects that turn out to be ill-advised in a changing society. Everyone runs this risk, particularly in time of war. Things learned or materials produced under the stress of war risk being judged to have been ill-advised after the bombs stop falling and the shooting is over. But chemists, like everyone else, are expected to respond to their society's needs of the moment and have no larger voice in how these needs evolve than do people in other walks of life.

What if after spending years on the way to qualify for a job or career in chemistry, I find chemistry is simply not my cup of tea? Fortunately, completing courses in chemistry can be a stepping-stone toward many other ways to earn a living. Medicine, nursing, dentistry, pharmacy, agriculture, metallurgy, architecture, and dietetics are some of the professions that require competency in chemistry, at least at the introductory level. Furthermore, chemists in training are usually required to do well in courses that support careers in chemistry, such as mathematics, computer technology, and communication skills. These courses can lead to careers other than chemistry.

When does all of this begin? It is never too late to set out to be a chemist. But the steps toward qualifying for chemistry-related jobs become more demanding as one climbs the education and training ladder. And particularly in chemistry, you are called on constantly to recycle and to build on what has been already learned.

BUT CHEMISTRY IS DIFFERENT

Even before taking the first steps along the way, there is something unique about chemistry that can have much to do with one's success. Chemistry is one of the few academic courses that combine general education with preparation for immediate employment. Completion of the high school chemistry course qualifies applicants for entry-level chemistry-related jobs. This affects how the course is taught and what teachers expect from their students. Students are expected to learn not only course content, but they are also to acquire a feel for who chemists are and what they do. This may cause the chemistry course to appear to be overly demanding, but it is also an advantage, particularly for young people who cannot afford the increasingly high cost of education beyond the high school level.

CHAPTER 1

LEARNING TO LIKE CHEMISTRY WHILE BECOMING GOOD AT IT

This chapter could just as well be titled, "Learning to Be Good at Chemistry While Learning to Like It." The point is that one depends upon the other. And neither is likely to happen unless we face up to several problems. For one, chemistry courses have long had the reputation of being very demanding. Only physics and mathematics are remembered by many people as being as intimidating. But little is gained by keeping this point of view alive. It makes better sense to look for reasons why chemistry courses may seem to be difficult, and then use each reason as a stepping-stone to success rather than as a detour to failure.

THE FIRST STEPPING-STONE: CHEMISTRY IS PROPERTIES

One of the first things to be learned in chemistry is so mundane that its importance is easily overlooked. It is the properties of substances, what they are and can do, that make them useful. Properties, in turn, are determined by the kinds, number, and arrangement of the atoms that make up their separate particles, usually molecules. This fundamental concept is easily missed when we are expecting chemistry to be difficult. Actually, this concept is the keystone that supports the entire chemistry enterprise. It is the first step toward seeing things that happen as being dependent upon the kinds of substances that are at hand and, in turn, on the properties of these substances. This concept is as essential to a child's appreciation of the bubbly froth that results when baking soda is sprinkled into vinegar as it is to an experienced chemist on his or her way to a Nobel award.

Let's take this concept a step further. There is an enormous challenge in the concept that what a substance is and what it can do depends upon its atomic makeup. Consider the world of amazingly useful substances that occur in nature. What is there to keep us from doing in glassware everything that occurs in nature? There is even greater challenge in bringing together new combinations of atoms in ways that yield substances whose properties will solve problems for which nature does not yet provide solutions.

THE SECOND STEPPING-STONE:
CHEMISTRY IS INVISIBLE

One big difficulty in chemistry is that we can't actually see what we want to do with things or to things. We can't count or weigh, turn end on end, touch, taste, or feel the actual building blocks of a substance we might want to create. We are like football coaches who are trying to come up with game-winning plays but who are so far from the playing field that all they can see or hear are blurs of color or dull thuds coming from shapeless masses moving about with no apparent reason.

In less metaphorical language, success in learning to like chemistry depends upon becoming able to "see" things that are too small to be visible, that have so little weight that they can be weighed accurately only if lumped together millions at a time, and that have architectural features that can only be imagined. But all of this doesn't keep us from becoming familiar with the behavior of nature's ninety or so atoms that are the players in chemistry's great game of taking things apart and putting things together.

THE THIRD STEPPING-STONE: CHEMISTRY IS RESHUFFLING

There are situations in chemistry where only our imaginations can take us from where we are to where we need to go. If we define a chemical as a unique combination of atoms sticking together to form discrete particles, everything under the sun is a chemical. Any substance, living or dead, on this or any other planet, is fair game to be taken apart and the fragments reassembled in new combinations. But it is misleading to imply that this is easy to do. Not always can we determine the makeup of nature's molecules that do wondrous things—or how to build new molecules that will have the properties required to solve a specific problem. Consider, for example, the things the human brain can do. It would require a fantastic imagination to design the kinds of molecules needed to build a system that can think, remember, and even conceive scenarios on its own while we are sleeping.

How this and the previous stepping-stones lead to career opportunities in chemistry is illustrated by the work of Dr. Donald J. Lyman, one of the chemists who helped make this book possible. In his words, "Since most things in life relate to molecules or aggregations of molecules (materials) and their reactions and interactions, chemistry does perform a very essential role... I attended a seminar at the Medical School of Stanford University and heard Dr. Belding Scribner (University of Washington) talk about the artificial kidney and the experience with the first ten or twelve patients. Dr. Scribner was the pioneer developer of the artificial system for chronic (continuous) dialysis. As Dr. Scribner talked, it seemed to me that many of the problems they were experiencing were related to the materials that were being used to make these new artificial kidney devices. That is, the membranes which help to separate the bad molecules out of the blood were not working as well as they might, and the blood contacting surfaces in the shunts and tubing were causing blood clots to form... That was 1962, and now, thirty two years later, I am still excited and actively pursuing answers to questions of how polymers and the body interact so that we can develop the best implants and artificial organs to save lives and improve health."

In nature's way of doing things, platelets in the blood initiate clotting immediately when they contact the surface of alien objects. Dr. Lyman realized that the inside surface of the tubing used to conduct blood during dialysis caused platelets to initiate clotting—a problem that could be solved if a plastic could be produced whose surface lacked the property of initiating clotting. Such a plastic eventually became available. Memories of this success prompt Dr. Lyman to say, "I think the excitement of the work comes from both exploring areas and trying the difficult experiments that many do not want to try for fear of failure. What should be learned is that one does not fail, but gains knowledge which helps one to better pose the next question."

In addition to constructing new molecules from the fragments of existing molecules, chemists also find success by adding to or redesigning nature's molecules. The work of Dr. Clive Elson at the St. Mary's University of Halifax is a good example. As reported in *Discover Canadian Chemistry* for October 1995, Dr. Elson begins with chitin molecules, a substance that occurs in many kinds of animals, particularly in the protective covering of crabs, shrimp, lobsters, crayfish, and similar critters.

Since chitin is one of nature's molecules, it is to be expected that it would be accepted by body tissues if it were used to repair damaged organs, particularly broken bones. The trouble is that chitin in its natural condition doesn't enter into the normal metabolism of bone formation and repair. Dr. Elson solved this problem by replacing one of the groups of atoms that make up the chitin molecule with a slightly different group of atoms. This change caused the new derivative to be soluble in body fluids and thereby able to enter into normal metabolic processes.

This new molecule can now be mixed with another substance to form a paste that will harden and reinforce a broken bone during the healing process. This paste also can be used to increase the healing rate of other kinds of body tissues. For a nonmedical use, this modified chitin is used to give certain kinds of fruits and vegetables a protective coating. By keeping oxygen out and carbon dioxide in, "shelf-life" is extended for several months.

THE FOURTH STEPPING-STONE: CHEMISTRY IS ENERGY

This brings us to another step on our way to becoming good at and enjoying chemistry. Energy plays an essential role in taking molecules apart and reassembling their fragments to form new combinations. But energy is difficult to understand. We recognize it only by what it does to matter when it changes from one form to another or flows from where there is much to where there is less. We know that energy is always either absorbed within the new molecules or radiated to the surrounding environment whenever a chemical change occurs.

Another of energy's characteristics is much more easy to observe than to explain. Energy seems always to be hell-bent to go from wherever it is to some place beyond our ken. An explosive example is what happens when the energy that holds nitroglycerine molecules together is allowed to escape. The energy in gasoline that ends up making wheels go around is a less destructive example. And there is the energy that holds together the large molecules of carbohydrates, fats, and proteins that make up our daily diet. This energy can by recycled either to form new body tissues, or to be changed to other forms to make muscles work or to keep us warm. All of this happens when energy is on its relentless journey to we are not sure where.

Chemists learn to measure the amount of energy that binds together the atoms in each kind of molecule and to predict how much energy is required to take a molecule apart. This includes allowing for energy that may "escape" during a reaction or is absorbed from outside. But energy keeps its secrets. This is particularly the case in life's chemistry, where there are many examples of energy seeming to delay its urge to arrive at the mysterious destiny we call entropy.

THE FIFTH STEPPING-STONE:
CHEMISTRY IS UNLIMITED

There is an expression that goes something like, "Don't give all of your attention to the trees or you may get lost in the forest." This suggests a problem that can not only keep beginners from liking and becoming good at chemistry, but can apply equally to experienced chemists. The fun in chemistry, the satisfactions that come with being good at chemistry, radiate more from the "forest" than from the "trees." There are so many chemicals in the world, there is so much to learn about how countless chemical events occur, that to try to take the whole of chemistry in one gulp is numbing.

Learning such things as the chemical names and formulas for everyday chemicals starts out being fun. And so does learning to balance a few chemical equations. But fun is likely to turn to boredom and a feeling of futility if such lessons are carried too far. It is important to keep in mind what chemistry really is and look forward to becoming able to do what chemists do. Each lab exercise or each classroom demonstration can be interesting in itself, but it is always wise to seek out the bigger ideas or concepts that may be involved.

Experienced chemists risk similar hazards. It is easy to become totally captivated by learning more and more about fewer and fewer chemicals or chemical events. Or to be driven to describe to the utmost degree of accuracy the properties of a single chemical. All of this is at the expense of keeping in mind how these properties might be used to solve society's problems. When this happens, careers or jobs in chemistry fall short of yielding the satisfactions that come with really enjoying and being good at chemistry.

THE SIXTH STEPPING-STONE: CHEMISTRY IS COOPERATION

All along the way toward a career in chemistry, things go best when teachers and their students respect each other in ways that strengthen everyone's capabilities and compensate for weaknesses. This helps everyone fulfill their hopes and ambitions. This is especially the case in chemistry. The high school chemistry course alone qualifies applicants for entry-level jobs in the chemical enterprise. Teachers keep this in mind when they set the standards for their courses. They want to know that those who complete the course are adequately prepared. To do otherwise would be as worrisome as allowing student drivers on highways—without having learned the rules of safe driving.

Another state of affairs often influences how chemistry teachers and their students feel about each other. Teachers tend to teach as they were taught. At the same time, they are often urged to explore new theories dealing with the what, how, and why of what they teach. Much is gained when teachers and students work together toward making the most possible out of both established and new ways to learn.

One suggestion applies directly to developing good relationships between students and their teachers. Always keep in mind that the heart of chemistry is the reshuffling of atoms from molecule to molecule. Two questions are very useful when a lesson seems to be going nowhere: What does this lesson have to do with how molecules can be taken apart? How can atoms or fragments of molecules be brought together to form new molecules?

Teachers like to have their students ask questions, but there is one kind of question that sometimes causes trouble. Although curiosity is the fuel that feeds science, asking *why* things happen can cause one's curiosity to fade away. There are no really satisfying answers to such questions as: If water is made up from the two gases—hydrogen and oxygen— why is water a liquid under most circumstances? It is unfair to think teachers make chemistry uninteresting because they can't answer such a question. A little story told by a widely recognized physicist bears on this. As a boy, he asked his father why a block castle built in a toy wagon would not fall over if the wagon was started moving very slowly. The father's answer was something like, "I don't know but isn't it interesting that this is always so?" Staying in the path that leads to careers in all of the sciences seems to call for being satisfied with simply describing with ever-increasing precision how things happen and leaving the why and wherefore to people in other professions.

Learning to notice things helps keep our curiosity alive. The color in soap bubbles. The symmetry of snowflakes. The aroma of baking bread or the fragrance of a gardenia. The solidity of an ice cube, the liquidity of water, the scalding temperature of steam. We are all born to be curious, but we must develop the habit of seeing things and asking ourselves questions.

THE SEVENTH STEPPING-STONE:
CHEMISTRY IS PARTICLES

Becoming familiar with the individual characteristics of each of nature's building blocks is a giant step along the way to jobs and careers in chemistry. Knowing the architecture of each kind of nature's ninety or so atoms makes it possible to understand much of what can be observed during chemical events. Some examples are: Why do some kinds of atoms tend to show a combining capacity of one to one while others combine in the ratio of one to two, two to three, three to four, but only rarely more complex than four to five? Why are some kinds of atoms most often found totally uncombined with any other kind of atom? Why do some kinds of atoms, in time, change their identity and become atoms of a totally different element?

Another valuable assist comes from recognizing how the members of families of the elements share similar characteristics, sometimes equally, other times changing in intensity with the increasing weight of each family member. All members of the halogen family, for example, tend to show a combining capacity of one, but each family member becomes increasingly dense as their weights increase.

THE EIGHTH STEPPING-STONE: CHEMISTRY IS COUNTING

Learning to send known numbers of atoms or molecules into a chemical reaction is a giant step toward becoming comfortable in chemistry. The difficulties associated with this step begin with the fact that the size and weight of individual atoms and molecules makes it impossible to count or weigh them directly. We can do this only indirectly by using the concept of relative weights. The relative weights of all kinds of atoms have been determined. For example, if we assign a weight of 1 to the hydrogen atom, the lightest of all atoms, it has been determined that carbon atoms are 12 times as heavy, oxygen atoms 16 times, and sodium atoms 23 times as heavy. On this basis, 23 grams of sodium, 1 gram of hydrogen, and 12 grams of carbon would contain equal numbers of atoms. Using similar reasoning, 48 grams of oxygen (3×16) would contain three times this number of oxygen atoms. Furthermore, if the formula for baking soda is $NaHCO_3$, then 84 grams of baking soda ($23 + 1 + 12 + [3 \times 16]$) would contain this same number of soda molecules.

The concept of relative weights makes it possible to bring together numbers of all kinds of molecules whose formulas are known. Here is an everyday example. Baking recipes usually call for a way to make the finished product spongy. Bubbles of carbon dioxide will do this, and when molecules of baking soda and vinegar interact, one of the products is gaseous carbon dioxide. But neither baking soda nor acetic acid, the active ingredient in vinegar, tastes good. Hence, no molecules of either should be left over, that is, for each molecule of baking soda in a recipe there must be one molecule of acetic acid, assuming that these molecules react on a one-to-one basis.

The formula of acetic acid, $C_2H_4O_2$, tells us that a molecule is made up from 2 carbon, 4 hydrogen, and 2 oxygen atoms. Their relative weights add to 60 ($[2 \times 12] + [4 \times 1] + [2 \times 16]$). Using the relative weight of a baking soda molecule as discussed above, we see that 84 grams of baking soda and 60 grams of acetic acid contain the same number of molecules. Recipes that call for these ingredients in the ratio of 84 grams to 60 grams will have neither left over to spoil the taste of the finished product.

Actually, using the concept of relative weights to count and weigh atoms and molecules isn't quite this simple. Not all of the atoms in an element weigh the same. The number of neutrons in an atom's nucleus can vary. This changes the weight but doesn't affect chemical properties. For example, some of nature's hydrogen atoms contain one or two neutrons. Since a neutron weighs essentially the same as a "normal" hydrogen atom, this doubles or triples the weight of these atoms. The presence of these higher weight "isotopes" gives hydrogen atoms as they occur in nature a relative average weight of 1.0078. This state of affairs applies to the atoms of all of the elements and explains why their relative weights are not whole numbers.

Catching onto the concept of relative weights is both the most important and the most elusive step on the way to learning to like and be good at doing chemistry. The use of this concept cuts across much of the arithmetic of chemistry. Here is one of the many examples. Suppose we do not know the formula of what appears to be a sample of iron ore. Analysis of a 160-gram sample yields 112 grams of iron and 48 grams of oxygen. Using the relative weights of iron and oxygen atoms as being 56 and 16, we see that the ratio of iron atoms to oxygen atoms is 2 to 3 (112/56 to 48/16). This tells us that the formula for this ore is Fe_2O_3. (To make this example easier to follow, we ignore the fact that there are isotopes of iron and oxygen atoms.)

There is more. It has been determined that the number of atoms in the relative weight of any kind of atom, if expressed in grams, is 6.02×10 to the 23rd power. This number enables us to determine the actual number of particles in a weighed sample of any element or compound of known formula. For example, a teaspoonful of baking soda (2 grams), can be determined to contain roughly 12×10 raised to the 20th power soda molecules (2 grams/84 grams per mole $\times$ 6×10 raised to the 23rd power). The term, mole, is a much used but somewhat confusing abbreviation for the number of atoms or molecules in the relative weight of an atom or molecule expressed in grams, this number being 6.02×10 raised to the 23rd power.

A FINAL STEP:
CHEMISTRY IS LABS AND DEMOS

The final step toward learning to like chemistry while becoming good at it involves making the most possible out of the two class formats that are used widely by chemistry teachers: classroom demonstrations and lab exercises. For some students, a colorful or noisy demonstration is nothing more than entertainment. For others, the same demonstration whets curiosity and the urge to find out the hidden causes of what they observe. For some, a demonstration triggers no more intellectual exercise than watching a science-related stunt being performed on a TV show. Others feel an intense urge to identify the chemical concepts or principles that the demonstration is expected to teach.

Laboratory exercises are usually approached enthusiastically, but they can also cause apprehension and frustration. It is good to know in advance the strategy that underlies a lab exercise. Some exercises help to add reality to seemingly vague concepts. Some recycle experiments performed many years ago, when a basic concept was first identified. Others are to practice lab skills or add reality to math applications.

Lab exercises designed to practice investigative skills can be both very rewarding and very demanding. Exercises of this type usually begin by confronting you with what is intended to be a puzzling observation, something that happens unexpectedly or is contrary to the way things usually happen. This assumes you have a backlog of experience with similar things happening in orderly, predictable fashion. If you lack such experience, it is wise to ask your teacher what you were expected to know in advance of this lab exercise.

The second phase of this type of lab exercise expects you to come up with tentative explanations for puzzling observations. This is an opportunity to retrieve and apply previously taught information. The more information you can recall, the greater the chances that your hypotheses will prove to be valid.

The third phase of this type of instruction calls for designing and carrying out experiments or investigations that will test the validity of your tentative explanation. At the elementary level, the design of an experiment is based on proving that the observed event cannot occur in the absence of what is thought to be the cause. Or that the observed event occurs every time the assumed cause is present. Or that variations in the magnitude of the assumed cause will always be accompanied by variations in the event under consideration. Practicing these strategies includes recognizing their shortcomings, such as failing to take into account the effects of unanticipated conditions or the possibility that several things may interact to become the actual cause of the event in question.

A sample demonstration and two representative lab exercises will help flesh out what is being said. For the demonstration, 20 g of ammonium chloride is put into a two-liter flask that is fitted with a one-hole rubber stopper and a delivery tube leading to the bottom of a three-liter beaker that contains two liters of water to which has been added phenolthalein. At this point the teacher announces that a small amount of water will be added to the ammonium chloride followed by 10 g of sodium hydroxide. The rubber stopper is to be replaced immediately, and each student is to record all observations deemed to be significant, but with no audible comments.

Representative observations are: Bubbles appeared in the water in the beaker. Pink color appeared at the opening of the delivery tube and spread throughout the water. Suddenly the water moved from the beaker over to the flask. At this point, the ban on conversation was lifted only to clarify observations. Then each student is to record his or her best explanation of what has been observed together with suggested experiments whereby each tentative explanation could be verified or abandoned.

The important question here is: How can one derive the most value and satisfaction while taking part in demonstration-centered lessons? Certain skills are self-evident. Things must be observed accurately and in detail. To shy away from things you cannot explain right away is foolhardy. And retrieving previously taught information is essential. For this sample demonstration, background information includes: Chloride and hydroxyl ions are negatively charged. The bond between sodium and chloride ions is more stable than the bond between ammonium and chloride ions. In a water environment, ammonium molecules can replace ammonium ions. Ammonia, a gas, displaces the air in the flask thus accounting for the bubbles. But ammonia is highly soluble in water and reacts to form ammonium ions, thus liberating hydroxyl ions whose presence is indicated by the action of the phenolthalein.

Some previously taught information goes back to general science classes. Atmospheric pressure is involved. When the ammonia in the flask is dissolved in the water initially in the beaker, air pressure on the water becomes greater than that inside the flask. A hard, cold fact is that success in chemistry depends very much on being able to retrieve and apply information and to know what information will take the mystery out of puzzling observations or add up to solutions to problems.

Success in the laboratory is pretty much up to each student. The following example assumes the teacher does nothing more than assign the exercise. Briefly stated, you are to leave a weighed length of copper wire hanging overnight in a solution of silver nitrate. On the next day, you are to shake loose the material that has collected on the wire, pour off the liquid, dry and weigh the wire, and dry and weigh the material that had collected on the wire. Further directions call for dividing the weight lost by the copper wire by the atomic weight of copper and the weight of the contents of the beaker by the atomic weight of silver.

The worst possible scenario describing participation in this lab exercise would leave you with all of the blanks in the printed lab report filled in properly but with no sense of having accomplished anything meaningful. This happens when lab exercises are carried out cookbook fashion without knowing what the recipes are supposed to yield. Remedies are easy to come by. You can always ask yourself, "What am I expected to learn from this exercise?" And a sympathetic teacher might suggest, "Here is an opportunity to use what you have been learning about the mole concept to discover for yourself that copper atoms have twice the combining capacity of silver atoms."

This lab exercise brings to mind many of the reasons why chemistry can be frustrating. It requires seeing things differently than we are accustomed to. Ordinarily, silver is a hard, shiny metal. We might accept such a name as silver nitrate, but it is quite a stretch of the imagination to envision silver particles suspended in a totally clear solution. And the finely divided silver that collected on the copper wire doesn't look like ordinary silver. Similarly, it is common knowledge that copper is a hard, copper-color metal. We know the copper wire lost weight, but it doesn't follow that the lost copper would be responsible for changing a solution from colorless to blue. It is equally mysterious that invisible silver particles in a solution would be replaced by copper particles simply by bumping into each other. Not to mention why one copper particle would replace precisely two silver particles. And who would guess that all of these mysterious things are supposed to help you count particles that are totally invisible!

A second lab exercise shows how things don't get any easier as you work your way toward a career in chemistry. Here you confront two flasks, each containing two immiscible clear liquids. Ten or so paper discs from a paper punch that are black on one side and white on the other are at the interface between the two liquids. You are to shake each flask vigorously and then allow the contents to settle. Upon doing so, you notice that the paper discs invariably end up with all of the black sides up in one flask and down in the other. The teacher may or may not identify the two liquids in each flask.

Accepting the challenge of accounting for the puzzling behavior of the paper discs, you bring to mind why two liquids don't mix or blend together. This leads to retrieving the concept of polarity, a property of solvents that traces to regions of positive or negative charge on their individual particles. Nonpolar solvents lack this property—a property that has much to do with the kinds of substances a solvent will dissolve. Then there is the rule that "like dissolves like," with the converse being that a polar solvent particle might repel a particle that is attracted by a nonpolar particle.

Teachers never know how long each student wants to go it alone, but in the case of this challenging lab exercise, there is a time when it would be appropriate to ask the student such a question as: "I wonder what there is in ink that might make it black?" To bring carbon to mind may be all it would take to alert the student to the differences between polar and nonpolar solvents. And this hint may be enough to enable the student to go the rest of the way toward enjoying the satisfaction of meeting the challenge that was posed by this lab exercise. But all is lost by giving up too soon.

TROUBLES ALONG THE WAY

There is something different about chemistry that can have much to do with one's success. It is one of the few academic courses that combines the goals of general education with preparation for immediate employment. Completion of the high-school-level chemistry course qualifies applicants for entry-level chemistry-related jobs. And this affects the way chemistry is taught and what teachers expect from their students. Teachers expect their students to learn not only what is in their textbooks but to also acquire a feel for who chemists are, what they do, and how they do it. This state of affairs is actually an advantage for young people who cannot afford the increasingly high cost of education beyond the high-school level. It is common practice for employers to help employees who do well at entry-level jobs to complete college or university-level courses. And this leads to unlimited advancement in the profession.

Fortunately, being aware of the unique demands of the first-level chemistry course is enough to enable one to earn the high grades they are accustomed to in other courses. But there is something more than learning to think like a chemist. The methods chemistry teachers use may be misleading. Chemistry lends itself to creating a wide array of audiovisual aids. Classroom demonstrations can be quite dramatic. Only the lack of appropriate furniture may keep students from becoming habitual "couch potatoes" in their chemistry classes.

SOME SPECIFIC PROBLEMS

Two young people who had been very successful in their first chemistry course were asked to think back through the year and recall some of the things that threatened their enthusiasm for chemistry. Here is what one person said: "My troubles with oxidation-reduction can illustrate one of my problems. Normally one would expect *reducing* to indicate a decrease in the number of electrons associated with a particle ... no, the chemist has to complicate things and make reduction the *gaining* of electrons. Normally one would expect oxidation potentials ($E°$) to be multiplied by the coefficients needed to balance the net oxidation-reduction reaction equation ... No way. Again the chemist boggles us. Normally, one would expect a spontaneous reaction to have a *negative* $E°$ value, to be consistent with the delta-G (free energy) rule on spontaneity ... No, for a spontaneous reaction the $E°$ is *positive,* and, once again, we are confused."

An equally successful student responded to the request to identify some qualms by saying: "The only problems that I can think of involve the inaccuracies of chemistry, and the fact that one does not *really* know how or why this or that occurs. For example, when we were on the topic of equilibrium systems, I tried to picture in my mind thousands of little molecules shooting about randomly and guessed that for every group of molecules splitting up in a unit of time, another group was forming from the split up fragments. I felt, however, that this was painfully inadequate; to prove that goings on were really happening required mathematics of such complexity that I chose to leave it well alone. True, I knew how to use the constant, K, but what irked me was the huge question mark hiding behind that constant K. I finally consoled myself with the conjecture that the mechanics of the constant equilibrium had something to do with the random probability and energetics of the particles.

"The same thing was true of Le Chatelier's principle. I knew how to use it, but *why* was it true? It seemed very natural and obvious that if one decreased the volume of an equilibrium system, the stress would be that of increased pressure, which could be relieved by something or other happening to the molecules to allow them to take up more space. But *why* does this happen? Sooner or later, I stopped asking myself this sort of perplexing question and took things for granted; but at the same time, I lost part of the interest, intrigue, and vitality of chemistry."

CHAPTER 2

IF YOU WANT TO BE
A REALLY RICH CHEMIST

The title of this chapter and the one to follow, "If You Want to Be a Much Appreciated Chemist," may be misleading. More often than not, chemists respond to both kinds of motivation. And either kind of motivation can lead to achieving either or both goals. Similarly, some chemists are interested primarily in describing as accurately as possible how and why chemical reactions occur and helping people to better appreciate the chemistry that goes on in and around us. Other chemists are equally interested in keeping people comfortable, healthy, and well nourished.

Consider, for example, how Fredric L. Buchholz, at the Dow Chemical Company, feels about his work on superabsorbent polymers. These substances soak up amazing amounts of water and form a rubbery gel. Their uses range from keeping moisture away from fiber optic cables to forming a watertight seal surrounding the new tunnel between England and France. A flake form of these materials is used to soak up water in snow-making machines for ski resorts.

Buchholz cites a much more widespread use. "Because of the large absorption ratio of superabsorbent polymers, diapers can contain less of the fluff that causes their bulkiness. Research on superabsorbent polymers for diapers may not sound glamorous, in fact, my work is sometimes the butt of jokes! But I think this work is important because millions of people can benefit from the results of my work. Just think, every day parents and their babies around the world are happier because of the work that I do. But I don't dwell on the usefulness of superabsorbent polymers. I enjoy this research because of the discoveries I make every day. Some of them are more useful than others, and some have been discovered before, but all of them make chemistry fun. Figuring out how or why something works adds a richness to discovery that I find very satisfying. Learning more about how substances behave adds another enjoyable dimension. My joy and satisfactions come from choosing projects that someone else finds useful. I have a rich career in chemistry by having fun understanding and solving problems that also interest other people."

Stepping aside from motivations, it does happen that some chemists become very rich. How this happens is straightforward, nothing that is magical or superhuman, although there is always the matter of chance favoring the prepared mind, or being at the right place with the right idea at the right time. Several steps seem to show through the stories of chemists who have reaped rich financial rewards from their careers. They may come in any sequence, but here are some of the steps that lead to high levels of dollar success:

1. Catch a glimpse of what it will take to solve an important problem or to improve an existing solution.
2. Assume that what is needed is a new product or the modification of an existing product.

3. Spell out in detail the chemical and physical properties of the requisite new material.
4. Anticipate health and safety precautions and how the production and distribution of the required product might impact the environment or exhaust the available supply of nature's raw materials and energy resources.
5. Make sure the new product can be produced and distributed profitably.
6. Determine if the new product will infringe on existing patents. Will it be patentable?

Francesco Bellini, president and chief executive officer of Canada's Biochem Pharma, Inc., offers advice on "How to Bring an Idea to Market," this being the title of a June 1994, article in the *Canadian Chemical News*. "Together with skilled and dedicated people, time, money and luck play a large part in taking ideas from the lab to the marketplace." Specifically, one of his employees, Bernard Belleau, caught the idea that the effectiveness of an available drug for AIDS could be improved by modifying the sugar ring portion of its molecules. The next step was to pull off the necessary chemistry. When adequate quantities of the remodeled drug were available, it had to be proved to be "as powerful as AZT on inhibiting replication of the AIDS virus and was almost nontoxic to human cells."

With the help of alliances with American and Canadian universities, research proved "that we had a good compound on our hands." From then on "bringing an idea to market," became a matter of meeting governmental regulations and financing production and distribution costs.

A SAMPLE OPPORTUNITY

Not yet is there a totally satisfactory solution to the problems people who wear prescription eyeglasses encounter when they must face bright sunlight. Nor is there a good solution to the problems that are caused by sun glare on vehicle windshields. Current solutions to these problems are expensive, not very adaptable, and, in general, subject to being improved. A possible solution is a spray-on material. Such a material would need to be transparent to an adequate amount of light and in no way distort vision. It would have to allow for being applied in varying amounts to adjust to the intensity of the glare and be readily removable when no longer needed. It must dry quickly and not smear easily. Nonflammable, nontoxic, and nonallergic are additional requisite properties.

As for finding or creating such a product, here things are more easily said than done. Here is where those who succeed in becoming rich part company with those who only dream of attaining wealth. But there are good reasons to believe that it pays to acquire a strong background of knowledge about how molecules are put together in general—and to be able to bounce back after repeated instances of disappointment from ideas that led only down blind alleys.

A SECOND OPPORTUNITY

The potholes that appear in streets and highways during extensive freezing and thawing may not suggest white coats and traditional laboratories. Nor does cement or asphalt come to mind when one thinks of potentially highly profitable chemicals. But potholes are very real and expensive problems. Furthermore, there is much concern about the deteriorating condition of the nation's highways, bridges, and other concrete structures. Enormous rewards await anyone who can come up with improved highway construction materials. And finding a solution to the pothole problem would be a good place to begin.

There is more here than straight chemistry. It may not be enough to look for ways to improve concrete and asphalt. The track record of current efforts to repair potholes tells us that the time has come to reach out for substances with totally different properties. And this brings us to another situation that stands in the way of becoming a very rich chemist. There is the ability to convince other people that a newly developed product will measure up to expectations. New solutions to old problems confront resistance, and particularly so if they render obsolete established attempts to solve a problem. All of which is to say that successful chemists benefit from developing good communication and interpersonal skills.

But what about the often told tales of chemists happening upon fabulously remunerative discoveries—chemists who haven't struggled through years of increasingly demanding courses in chemistry and related subjects. This can happen, but we are not always told how many years of private study or how many setbacks and disappointments were omitted from such stories.

Some chemists say it is misleading to play up their profession as a way to become very rich. Quoting a former director of research for a major pharmaceutical company,

"More than 90 percent of chemists are employed by corporations, so the results of their efforts will not lead to fortunes. The corporation will pay their salary and bonus whether or not they make a *rich* discovery. They can only become rich by promotion to supervisory roles or to management positions where they can take advantage of bonuses or stock options. It is a different situation, of course, for chemists who are on university faculties. We made a number of academic inventors multimillionaires by licensing their patented inventions."

Motivations, of course, are personal, but we can say that the urge to make one's life count for something, to be successful financially, and to be appreciated are not at cross-purposes for those who choose chemistry for their career. The examples that follow will flesh out this point of view.

BUILD A PLACE TO LIVE AND THEY WILL COME

Several sets of circumstances are brought together in research headed by Dr. Kent S. Price at Delaware University's Graduate College of Marine Studies. First, the bulk of eighty million tons of coal ash waste generated by electric power plants annually ends up in landfills at a cost of as much as $15 per ton. Second, certain marine environments would support larger populations of desirable species of fish if they could find suitable places where they could build nests and be protected from predators. Third, there would also be the need to improve the environment in ways that support the growth of the plants and animals the fish feed on.

Dr. Price's research began with finding the best recipe for a type of concrete-based cinder block that would last indefinitely under seawater and attract colonies of marine life. Three promising recipes were developed. With the help of engineering consultants, concrete was stirred into coal ash and allowed to cure in one-foot-thick slabs. The cured slabs, in turn, were cut into irregular blocks roughly the size of a large filing cabinet and dumped into an appropriate test site in the Delaware Bay.

Seven weeks later, divers found a full growth of marine life flourishing on the artificial reef, including such desirable species as black sea bass and flounder. Divers returned to the site regularly to determine which recipe produced the blocks that best withstood erosion and attracted the greatest growth of marine life. It is to be particularly noted that this solution solved several problems at the same time, something that seems to be characteristic of chemistry.

EVERY ENEMY HAS A WEAKNESS

The work of Dr. J. Herbert Waite at this same research facility shows another feature of how some chemists attack problems. This problem began in 1988 when the zebra mussel found its way to the Great Lakes of North America. Unfortunately, it brought none of its natural predators with it. Since one zebra mussel can produce as many as 50,000 eggs each year, this threat to the environment expanded explosively. All available surfaces soon became covered with thick clusters of mussels. The intake pipes used to draw water from the lakes were particularly vulnerable. Engineers believed this form of environmental pollution would cost $5 billion during the 1990s alone. The cost of starving out native species of aquatic life would be even greater.

As yet, no window of opportunity has opened through which this threat can be attacked. All the easy efforts have failed. Those who are seeking to solve this problem are forced to explore all factors that might lead to the control of the zebra mussel's growth and survival rate. This includes describing, molecule by molecule, each action that enables the mussel to do what it does so efficiently. One such action produces an adhesive that cements its shell to an appropriate support. Dr. Waite believes this is where the mussel can be brought under control. He has described six kinds of molecules that build the tiny threads that are spun, one at a time, by the mussel's foot; these threads then splay out into an amazingly permanent adhesive that completes attachment to a supporting surface.

Dr. Waite describes these tiny threads as being "devoid of any living cells, are as strong as nylon, are synthesized and assembled in two to five minutes under water, and ultimately discarded as biodegradable waste." In effect, Dr. Waite is able to enter a chemical laboratory that is no larger than a tiny thread and can visualize interactions among at least six kinds of molecules. Some of these interactions occur in many steps. When this kind of information is published, other researchers will gain a valuable assist in joining Dr. Waite in seeking increasingly promising hypotheses whereby the zebra mussel may be brought under control.

EVERYTHING FROM SMELLY FISH
TO BLUE JEANS

Recent issues of the magazine, *Chemtech,* bring to mind the wide range of things chemists do not so much because they want to become very rich or be appreciated, but because of what chemistry is. The examples that follow have been chosen pretty much at random.

In the article, "Keeping the Drug in Your Eye," G. Gurtlier and his colleagues at the University of Geneva in Switzerland, describe the development of plastic inserts that delay the escape of drugs that are applied to the moist surfaces of the eye. Rather than administering eyedrops up to six times a day, less frequent doses become equally effective, and the surrounding eye tissues suffer less damage. This article appeared in the April 1995 issue.

Malvina Farcasier at the U.S. Department of Energy in an article titled, "Another Use for Old Tires," describes a way to reduce environmental pollution and, at the same time, add to the nation's supply of liquid fuels. The millions of old tires that are spilling over and sometimes catching fire in landfills are to be ground up, mixed with powdered coal, and converted to a liquid fuel.

Abdul Gaffer, John Afflitto, and Nuran Nabi at the Colgate-Palmolive Technology Center report devoting much research to finding out what chemistry goes on in one's mouth. In their article, "Toothbrush Chemistry," they tell how they developed triclosan, a product they believe will greatly lower the $5 to $6 billion annual cost of removing plaque.

Douglas L. Marshall at Louisiana State University in the article, "Nobody's Nose Knows," tells of studying the substances that cause stale fish to smell bad. He then developed an odor detecting method that is more sensitive than the human nose.

Another article, "What Makes That Coffee Smell So Good?," is based on Thomas H. Parliment and Harold D. Stah's identification of more then 800 compounds that contribute to the aroma that results from roasting green coffee beans. These researchers are with Kraft Foods, and the article appeared in the August 1995 issue.

Nontoxic, beadlike pills that absorb medications and gradually allow them to diffuse in time-release fashion are described by Cherng-ju Kim, of Temple University's School of Pharmacy, in "Hydrogel Beads for Oral Drug Delivery."

Hermann Goehna at Lurgi AG in Germany used his extensive study of catalysis to help solve two interrelated problems: Air pollution caused by excessive carbon dioxide, and how to maintain an adequate supply of liquid fuels. "Producing Methanol from CO_2" is the title of his article.

Using newly developed ways to transfer genes from one species to another, H. Maelor Davies at Calgene Chemicals is developing a cooking oil that keeps the best qualities of several kinds of oil. In "Designer Oils," he reports how he brings together the best genes from castor, canola, palm, and rapeseed oil. Whichever species grows most efficiently will then be used to produce the genetically improved oil.

Radioactive tracer molecules that enable research people to determine step by step how medications influence body processes are discussed by N. Satyamorthy, Joseph R. Barrio, and Mohammad Namavari in "Making 18F-radiotracers for Medical Research." This research team at the University of California at Los Angeles reports that these tracer molecules can be used to obtain very valuable diagnostic information.

"Come Up and See My (Ecologically Safe) Etchings," is the title of an article by Omri M. and Marion R. Bohr. These artists developed environmentally safe substitutes for the usual nitric acid method for etching zinc and copper. Their knowledge of electroplating enabled them to avoid allowing pollution hazards to interfere with carrying out their artistic urges.

While at Proctor and Gamble's Food and Beverage Technology Division, R. J. Jandacek believed that people could control their fat intake and not give up foods that were appealing. In his article, "Developing a Fat Substitute," he discusses the development of *olestra*. He came up with this product, which is not broken down by pancreatic lipase, after studying how fats are hydrolyzed. As it happens rather often with this kind of new product, not yet can we say how well it will be accepted by the general public.

In the article, "Color Yes; Cancer No," Harold S. Freeman traces research based on the hypothesis that molecules of potentially carcinogenic food dyes can be remodeled in ways that eliminate the cancer-causing property but do not interfere with their use of dyes. This research team worked at the North Carolina State University.

"Chemistry on a Stick," by E. Diebold, M. Papkin, and A. Usmani of Boehringer Mannheim Diagnostics, discusses very convenient ways to estimate what kind and how much of a specified substance is in one source or another. Multistep chemical actions are built into layers of reagents on an appropriate support material. Enzymes play major roles in the analytical procedures.

David Benson and Ed Tracy of the Solar Energy Research Institute believe something can be done to reduce the demand for air-conditioning on sunny days. They focus on the two billion square miles of windows in the United States and have developed a switchable electrochromatic film that can be made more or less opaque by low-voltage devices that respond to variations in light intensity. "Electrochromic, Sun-Control Windows," is the title of their article.

The article, "Better Bicycles Using Metal Matrix Composites," is of special interest to people who want their bicycles to be lightweight and very strong. David Lundy of the U.S. International Trade Division describes a structural material in which a metal or an alloy base is reinforced by a second material, usually ceramic.

The article, "Jeans Chemistry," by Tony Travis, is an example of chemistry being interestingly worthwhile in various ways. The author traces the growth of synthetic indigo until its use as a dye was almost abandoned. Then in the 1960s, fashion changes made faded jeans more popular, and the demand for synthetic indigo increased. Dr. Travis is at the Sidney M. Edelstein Center for the History and Philosophy of Science, Technology, and Medicine at the Hebrew University of Jerusalem.

CHAPTER 3

IF YOU WANT TO BE A MUCH APPRECIATED CHEMIST

Only rarely are chemists applauded openly for what they do. Theirs is an offstage, or supporting, role in improving the quality of life for the world's people. Or, using another metaphor, chemists more often score assists rather than make the winning touchdown or save the game by tagging out the runner as he or she comes crashing onto home plate. And no better example comes to mind than the use of air bags to save lives during potentially fatal collisions on our streets and highways.

AIR BAGS: WHERE CHEMISTRY SCORED AN ASSIST

The story begins as far back as the early 1950s when John W. Hedrick narrowly avoided crashing into a large rock that had fallen on the highway. When his auto veered toward a deep ditch along the road, both he and his wife used their arms to protect their young daughter. No one was injured in this accident, but it set Hedrick thinking that something could certainly be done to reduce the highway casualty rate.

He recalls having seen so many car accidents, so many sheet-covered victims, many horribly mangled.

With this motivation, he set out to invent what came to be called the *air bag*. By 1953, he received a patent on an air bag that relied on compressed-air-inflating bags on the steering wheel hub, atop the dashboard, on the glove-box door, and inside the front seat-backs. In case of a collision, spring-loaded weight sensors would trigger the inflation process. Hedrick found no takers for his invention among automobile manufacturers, and the only satisfactions gained from his efforts came from knowing that the major manufacturers assigned engineers to look for better solutions to the auto safety problem.

During the next twenty or so years, millions of dollars and many hours were spent on efforts to solve the problems that kept air bags from becoming generally accepted. A major contribution that came during the late 1960s gives us an example of chemists scoring an essential "assist." Many of the defects in the experimental models of air bags involved storing adequate amounts of compressed air and having it inflate the air bag within a matter of milliseconds. By now, however, chemists working for the aerospace industry had developed a way to inflate bags by detonating an explosive that produced a large volume of nitrogen.

This solution to design problems had much in its favor. The necessary explosive could be prepared in pellets and stored in a small container. The burning rate could be adjusted to allow an adequate volume of nitrogen to be produced in less time than it would take for the auto's occupants' bodies to be propelled into the steering wheel or instrument panel following a crash. And nitrogen is neither toxic, flammable, or corrosive. All that was needed to inflate the air bag was an electrical signal triggered by sensors located on the parts of an automobile most likely to make contact when a collision occurred.

The success of this chemistry-related project can be shown in several ways. Exactly how many lives are being saved by air bags cannot be determined. But just as it took the risks involved in the lives of only one family to trigger the entire project, to save a single life is a wonderfully rich reward. And from another point of view, sales of the essential explosive amounted to an estimated annual net income of $269 million for the major supplier.

THE ADVANTAGES OF TEMPERED GLASS

How chemists score assists is also illustrated by the work of Dr. S. S. Kistler while he was at the University of Utah. His work began with two seemingly unrelated observations. First, the properties of glass make it useful in many ways, but it breaks fairly easily. Second, if a board that is to be used as a footbridge is kept stressed in an upward curved condition, it is less likely to break under a heavy load. Kistler built these observations into an hypothesis: Glass would be less breakable if the outer layers of its makeup were kept under stress. Calling on background knowledge, he knew that ordinary glass is made by melting a mixture of sand, lime, and soda ash. Glass that is transparent, though breakable, is produced when a batch of these raw materials is heated to an adequately high temperature. Dr. Kistler also knew that the actual building blocks that make glass are silicate, calcium, and sodium ions.

At this point, some very elementary chemical concepts come into play. Sodium is in the same chemical family as potassium, and thus the two elements share similar properties. But potassium ions are larger than sodium ions. A second, equally basic concept tells us that there is constant motion within and between all kinds of molecules with the degree of motion being dependent upon temperature. Putting these and other concepts together, and adding the elusive ingredient we call creativity, Dr. Kistler came up with a way to put the outer layers of the particles that make up glass under stress: Simply allow the larger potassium ions to squeeze into the spaces formerly occupied by sodium ions.

This is what a team of scientists at Corning Glass managed to do. They heated potassium nitrate to its melting temperature in a stainless steel tank. At this temperature, vibration produces reasonably wide spaces between the potassium and nitrate ions. Ordinary glass is then lowered into the melted potassium nitrate. As the temperature of the glass rises, its sodium ions vibrate more extensively. This creates opportunities for sodium and potassium ions to exchange positions. After approximately sixteen hours of this action, enough sodium and potassium ions have displaced each other that when the glass cools, the outer layers will be stuffed with the larger potassium ions thus producing the required stress.

Do-It-Yourself Hypodermics

One of the uses of this tempered glass illustrates how chemistry's offstage role gives reasons for chemists to be appreciated. The story begins during the early 1950s, when it was feared that military personnel, and civilians as well, might be subjected to fatal nerve gas attacks. Although a protective medication was available, it had to be injected immediately upon sensing symptoms of being exposed to the toxic gas. All military personnel who were likely to be under attack were supplied with a syrette, a toothpaste-type collapsible tube fitted with a hypodermic needle and containing a dose of the medication. If exposed to nerve gas, the victim was expected to remove the protecting cover, jab the needle into the thigh, and roll up the tube in order to force the medication into the muscle.

Field trials of these syrettes under simulated battle conditions yielded terribly dismal results. Many wanted no part of the whole idea. Some people fainted during the process of injecting themselves. There had to be a better way. At this point, a research team composed of scientists and engineers at Survival Technology Incorporated (STI) began looking for this better way. Soon the team came up with a spring loaded auto-injector using a metal cartridge to contain the required medication. The spring was strong enough to drive the needle through several layers of clothing and to propel the medication through the opening of a fine-bore needle. Victims of nerve gas exposure could medicate themselves within seconds after feeling symptoms without seeing and only scarcely feeling the needle.

But here were serious shortcomings. As new medications were introduced to treat newly developed nerve gas threats, some medications were degraded by being exposed to the metal in the cartridge. Furthermore, the cartridge had to be large enough to allow the newer medications to be diluted sufficiently to avoid damaging tissues at the point of injection. At the same time, the cartridge had to withstand rough treatment and protect against premature or accidental discharge. This is where tempered glass entered the story. Making the cartridge out of specially tempered glass rather than metal kept the medication effective. And the tempered glass was sufficiently rugged.

From the Gulf War to Bee Stings

Soon after these autoinjectors were proved to be effective for use in the military, civilian doctors realized they could save lives where treatment required immediate self-administration of an accurately measured dose of an appropriate medicine. Anaphylactic shock is one example. This sudden allergic reaction to an insect sting or to a food or medicine can result in death within minutes. Epinephrine is the drug of choice for emergency treatment. Quoting an advertisement recommending the use of epinephrine auto-injectors, "patients can have epinephrine with them for immediate self-administration, should the need arise ... simply remove the safety cap and press black tip against thigh to deliver an accurate, premeasured intramuscular dose ... Injection may be made directly through clothing if necessary. The concealed needle minimizes fear and resistance to self-injection."

Fear of nerve gas attacks was very real during the Gulf War. All U.S. personnel carried autoinjectors loaded with appropriate protective medication. Although no occasions required their use, having this protection against nerve gas attacks did much toward maintaining troop morale. In fact, STI proudly displays a plaque testifying to being much appreciated for what the company did to ensure the success of the United States in the Gulf War. Only a few of the people who see this plaque, however, will know of the role Dr. Kistler played in making possible what the plaque represents. Nor will the people whose lives may be saved by heading off anaphylaxis be able to thank him.

GOVERNMENT-SPONSORED OPPORTUNITIES

Government agencies make available many opportunities for chemists who are specially attracted by careers that combine public service and chemistry. The U.S. Department of Agriculture is a good example of such agencies. One of its publications, *Agricultural Research,* provides brief reviews of research projects of special interest to the public. Examples follow.

Fifteen men who volunteered to try out a selenium-rich diet for fifteen weeks enabled James G. Penland and Lori Matthys to investigate the hypothesis that one's mood is affected by how much of this element is consumed daily. Their work at the Human Nutrition Research Center at Grand Forks, North Dakota, revealed that these men, when compared with a control group, "felt more agreeable than hostile, more clearheaded than confused, more composed than anxious, and more energetic than tired."

Another project began when the German government ruled that no sunflower kernels could be imported if they contained more than 0.3 parts per million of cadmium. This posed a threat to the $25 to $30 million U.S. growers received annually from the German market. One solution to this problem was to convince the German government to raise the limit to 0.6 parts per million. Rufus L. Chaney, of the Beltsville Environmental Chemistry Laboratory, approached the problem in a different way. He found that although cadmium as a trace metal occurs naturally in all soils, there are ways to reduce the amount of cadmium that is actually taken from the soil by sunflowers.

Merle F. Vigil of the Central Great Plains Research Station in Akron, Colorado, investigated ways to reduce the level of environmental pollution that results from the use of excessive amounts of fertilizers, particularly, nitrogen. He found that the generally accepted tests for the amount of nitrogen to be added to the soil did not take into account all of the factors that either remove or add nitrogen. Vigil and his colleagues developed a computer program that includes these factors.

This next project has wide implications. First, it was noted that cattle and sheep that grazed freely on a certain kind of weed in seven western states would sometimes become severely ill and die—but only if they ate too much. The key ingredient seemed to be the amount of oxalates consumed. And some cattle and sheep were much more susceptible than others. Milton J. Allison and Albert L. Baetz of the National Animal Research Unit in Ames, Iowa, traced the origin of this situation to the presence or absence of a kind of bacterium that is capable of breaking down oxalates. With the help of Peter Maloney, a microbiologist at The Johns Hopkins University, they found that this bacterium lives in the digestive tracts of cattle, sheep, and humans. In fact, this research takes on added importance because oxalates have been known to play a role in the formation of kidney stones in humans.

There are millions of people in the United States who cannot drink regular milk. They lack the lactase enzyme that breaks down lactose, the major type of sugar in milk. Virginia H. Holsinger and her colleagues at the Dairy Products Research Unit in Philadelphia, Pennsylvania, developed ways to add lactase to previously dried dairy products. When these products were reconstituted by replacing the water, the lactose is broken down and no longer poses a problem. This research had other important results. It led to a "spray-dried, free-flowing dehydrated butter powder that can replace conventional shortening... It gives a delectable butter flavor to cakes, pie crusts, and other baked goods when used in dry bakery mixes." And it poses no problem for people who are lactose intolerant.

The work of Donald T. Wicklow and Patrick F. Dowd of the Mycotoxin Research Unit of the National Center for Agricultural Utilization Research in Peoria, Illinois, provides another glimpse of the wide array of chemistry-related job opportunities in government agencies. Their project begins with knowing that although many kinds of insects feed on fungi, fungi manage to survive. This leads to the possibility that fungi produce the equivalent of insecticides. This, in turn, suggests that fungi may be the source of new insecticides that would pose no risk to the environment. In turn, Wicklow and Dowd isolated sclerotia, tiny fungal bits that look like black pepper, from more than 200 different fungi. Already these sclerotia show promise of being developed into effective and environmentally friendly insecticides.

CHEMISTRY OFFERS
UNLIMITED OPPORTUNITIES

There are no limits to the hopes and ambitions to be exercised in chemistry-related jobs and careers. And there are problems to be solved that offer challenges to the most dedicated and determined of investigators. From this point of view, there is much to be learned from the men and women who devote their lives to seeking solutions to humanity's most elusive problems. At some point in their careers, they seem to become totally committed to solving a problem, particularly if they believe they have caught a glimpse of a possible solution. From then on it is pretty much a matter of testing one hypothesis after another and, in doing so, accumulating a vast store of knowledge and knowhow, But there is something more. They learn to live with the discouragement and heartache that comes with setbacks from being led astray by disappointing hypotheses.

THE ADDICTION PHENOMENON

What is being said here can be fleshed out by using the problem of drug addiction, "the compulsive uncontrolled use of habit-forming drugs beyond the period of medical need or under conditions harmful to society." Dr. Nathan B. Eddy and Dr. Everette L. May are among the many men and women who know very well what it means to devote one's life to seeking a solution to a very elusive problem. One glimpse of possible success that motivated them came from within the morphine molecule. They believed it might be possible to remove a portion of the molecule and thereby eliminate the addiction-causing property but not diminish morphine's ability to relieve pain. And even more important, they wished to prove that drug addiction is caused by specific kinds of or fragments of molecules.

Morphine has a long history. Its use traces to curiosity about how opium, a drug that is obtained from poppy seed pods, relieves aches and pains. Early research learned how to separate a crystalline substance that is responsible for opium's drug effects. This is morphine, an effective pain-killer but as addictive as opium. Morphine was first prepared in 1803. Attempts to eliminate its addictive property began immediately. By 1947 it was known that each morphine molecule is built from 17 carbon, 19 hydrogen, 1 nitrogen, and 3 oxygen atoms. By 1923 chemists knew how all of these atoms fit together to form the morphine molecule.

Along the way to obtaining this information, morphine was treated with various kinds of molecules. In one case, two hydrogen atoms in the morphine molecule were replaced by portions of two molecules of the active ingredient in vinegar—acetic acid. This produced heroin. Heroin retained morphine's pain relieving and tranquilizing properties. Although morphine continues to be relied upon for relief of pain, not yet has its addictive property been eliminated. The same is true for heroin. Years of frustration have forced Dr. May to entertain the possibility that addiction to morphine or heroin is behavior that can be only partially caused by the chemistry of these molecules.

What Dr. May suggests here is vitally important to anyone who is contemplating a career in chemistry, particularly in the field of health maintenance. He raises the question: At what point is human behavior, both physical and mental, influenced by actions that cannot be traced to interactions among the molecules of the substances that make up and circulate throughout our bodily tissues? Can there be as yet unidentified forces or forms of energy that determine when we are hungry, tired, depressed, happy, angry, sick, sexually aroused? Are there actions in nature that are more subtle than gravity, more adhesive than the attraction between electrically charged objects? Can it be that such forces come into play when we dream or reminisce, intellectualize, emotionalize, or experience creativity and inventiveness, forces that can be beamed from here to there and need no transmitting medium or pass through barriers even more easily than do those that transmit radio and television programs?

Yes, raising questions such as these can be seen as keeping company with charlatans who all too often proclaim their ability to use alien forms of energy to control the behavior of other people. On the positive side, there is more to be lost by closing rather than keeping one's mind open, even for things that seem to be outrageous at the time. And there is always the question of what to do when we are confronted with situations that conventional hypotheses simply cannot handle.

One such problem is the so-called placebo effect. It is standard practice to prove whether a medication cures a disease or remedies a dysfunction by conducting trials in which patients are given either the medicine or a placebo. Those who receive the medication are to differ in no significant way from those who receive the equivalent but nonmedicinal dosage. All too often, a significant fraction of those who receive the placebo show compelling evidence of reacting exactly as do their counterparts who received the actual medication. This state of affairs is of special concern to those who look forward to a career in pharmaceutical chemistry.

Drug addiction, an equally challenging problem, is increasingly being seen as biopsychosocial in origin. To be sure, addiction begins only with introducing specific kinds of alien molecules into body tissues either by way of ingesting or injecting. The initial effects are strictly chemical. Addiction, however, is a subsequent effect in which psychological and sociological actions may well influence and be influenced by the initial biochemical and physiological effects.

Because the addiction problem cuts across biology, psychology, physiology, and sociology, it is a very challenging problem. There is something here that is peculiarly challenging, something that was alluded to by Dr. Albert Szent-Gyorgi, one of America's great chemists: "As for myself, I like only basic problems, and could characterize my own research by telling you that, when I settled at Woods Hole and took up fishing, I always used an enormous hook. I was convinced I would catch nothing anyway, and I thought it much more exciting not to catch a big fish than not to catch a small one."

And drug addiction is a very "big fish." Not only because of the number of people who suffer from it, but for what it does to its victims. At first, taking drugs may be seen as a way to better manage one's life, to be one's own person, to control mood and emotions, to relieve anxiety and stress. After becoming addicted, everything is turned around. Drug addicts are reduced to puppets with an uncontrollable urge for another dose pulling at the strings. There is no longer any sensitivity to customary pleasures, no capacity to experience true happiness, no satisfactions to be gained from setting one's own goals.

The biopsychosocial nature of drug addiction adds a new dimension for those who would take on the challenge of bringing it under control. What is added is the ability to sell people in other professions on what chemistry is and can do and, in exchange, gather from other people what they know about why people behave as they do. As we point out in Chapter 11, "Chemistry Yesterday, Today, and Tomorrow," the very dimly seen link between the properties of molecules and why people act as they do is one of the most exciting topics on the frontiers of chemistry.

The addiction problem in connection with the use of tobacco illustrates something more to keep in mind when considering where a career in chemistry can go. Conflicting interests disagree on the addictive property of nicotine. This disagreement has produced an enormous amount of information dealing with the addiction phenomenon. Nicotine molecules seem to affect the brain in ways that cause people to want to experience the effect repeatedly. The apparent feelings of pleasure overpower all messages the brain may receive saying that experiencing this pleasure may be at the expense of a long and healthy life.

Lois R. Ember in an article titled, "The Nicotine Connection," in the November 28, 1994, issue of *C & EN* reports on research that follows nicotine molecules in great detail as they find their way to act on the neurons that apparently interact to produce feelings of pleasure as it is experienced normally. In effect, whatever it is that causes one to feel good when good things happen can be triggered artificially by the arrival of nicotine molecules. That a molecule could have such a fantastic property certainly stretches one's imagination. But this may point to one of the traits that bring success to chemists.

Yes, the drug addiction problem tests the imaginative ability. There are no psychological or sociological circumstances that, alone, can cause or prevent addiction. People everywhere in the world, in all walks of life, old and young, rich and poor, secure and insecure, loved and unloved, can become addicted. The only thing known for sure is that in all cases addiction begins with the ingestion or injection of molecules that have the properties required to cause addiction.

A HAPPIER VIEW OF CHEMISTRY

There is another, and much more pleasant way for chemists to enhance the quality of our lives. By learning to envision things at the molecular level, we can add a whole new degree of appreciation of the world around us. A beautiful example is the magnificent display of colors that appears each autumn on forest-covered hillsides in many parts of the country. For all too many people, this phenomenon evokes no deep appreciation, nothing beyond recalling childhood stories of Jack Frost's paintbrush. Chemists, too, enjoy recalling childhood memories, they also gain satisfactions by looking beyond the immediately observable and seeing the fantastic rearrangements of atoms within molecules that are taking place within the tissues of what were once green leaves.

As summer fades into autumn, there are wonderful examples of the chemistry of life responding to ever-changing environmental conditions. It is curious how different species within the same environment show such dissimilar patterns of changing colors. And how different twigs on the same tree may change color at different times. In fact, the more closely we observe this example of nature's chemistry, the better we appreciate how dependent the living world is on the physical environment.

Particularly puzzling is why trees and shrubs along highways show autumn color changes after being sprayed with weed killer. Or why wires twisted into the bark of maple tree branches will cause autumn color changes even in the middle of summer. Or why leaves on branches below a street light retain their green color weeks after those above the light have completed their autumn color changes. The point here is that with added knowledge comes improved ability to see things. And the better we see things, the more our curiosity is exercised. We have already identified an active curiosity as the first requisite toward a satisfying career in chemistry.

Here is a particularly thought-provoking example. While studying the chemistry of autumn leaf coloration, a high school student believed she caught glimpses of a mysterious "aging" hormone that accumulates in the tissues of green leaves during the growing season. She was puzzled to see so many kinds of perfectly healthy plants age and die, with no apparent reason that could be traced to unfavorable environmental conditions. She was well aware of how hormones can cause remarkable changes in her own body processes. Nothing may ever come from her hypothesis. But the ability to generate hypotheses will always be a vital step toward a successful career not only in chemistry but in all of the sciences.

PLANT CELLS FOR TOMORROW'S TEST TUBES

Even before there were such things as test tubes, people relied on substances that are produced by nature's chemistry to treat a wide variety of ailments and diseases. Elixirs were prepared from the leaves, roots, flowers, or fruits of plants that were known to have medicinal value. Dr. N. Towers of the University of British Columbia has developed a way to bring this kind of pharmaceutical chemistry up-to-date. His research team determines which tissues in a medicine-producing plant are most responsible for producing the active substance. Samples of these tissues are then reproduced by way of tissue culture, rather than having to grow the entire plant.

Already large enough samples of a compound that is derived from the common marigold have been produced to prove that this compound will prevent the reproduction of certain disease-causing viruses. There is more about Dr. Tower's work in the October 1995 issue of *Discover Canadian Chemistry.*

CHAPTER 4

EDUCATIONAL REQUIREMENTS

For some people, their interest in chemistry goes back to that first chemistry set that came as a birthday or holiday gift. For others, the idea of chemistry as a career came much later, even after spending much time earning their living in some other way. Thus, the path to chemistry-related jobs and careers is always open. Generally speaking, however, the educational requirements begin with the high school chemistry course and continue as far up the educational ladder as one wishes to go.

Much has been said about the individual attitudes and skills one is expected to develop while enrolled in the introductory chemistry course. From a more general point of view, one's first instruction in chemistry combines the fun and excitement of seeing chemical events occur with the discipline of learning the principles and concepts that are involved in taking things apart and putting things together. A lesson may feature seeing a colorful precipitate appear suddenly when two perfectly colorless solutions are combined, but the point of the lesson may be learning how temperature or some other factor influences the rate of a reaction.

Similarly, a lab exercise may call for weighing as accurately as possible the reactants and controlling the conditions that affect the rate at which the reaction occurs. But underlying all of the obvious things that are to be done is the intellectual challenge of constructing a mental model of the key atoms in the molecules that are reshuffled during the reaction. In other words, one must learn to do what is to be done and, at the same time, keep in mind what chemistry is really all about.

Students who do well when they "come out for" chemistry seem to respond very much like successful candidates who come out for sports. Making the football team, for example, calls for taking the bruises and the sometimes harsh discipline that is a part of the game and not letting that interfere with learning the fundamental strategies of football. There can be as much satisfaction in learning to use one's wits to outsmart atoms and molecules as ball carriers gain from outsmarting tacklers.

MATHEMATICS AND CHEMISTRY

On the good news side, being good at mathematics helps people advance toward successful careers in chemistry. The bad news is that there is enough mathematics in chemistry to cause people who expect all math to be frustrating to not be disappointed. The best news of all is that chemistry courses can improve attitudes toward math. Here is a wonderful opportunity to not only become familiar with quantitative relationships but to realize how useful they can be.

Keeping track of each quantitative skill you learn as you study chemistry can be the equivalent of a life support system. Use a special notebook to keep a running record of each math skill you become increasingly comfortable with. And don't be too proud to begin with addition and subtraction, multiplication and division, and other equally basic ways to deal with quantitative relationships. Include the ability to handle both regular and decimal fractions with and without the aid of a pocket calculator. Use each new lesson in your math courses to add new skills or new applications of previously acquired skills even before you need them in your chemistry class.

Don't hesitate to ask your math teachers to help you pin down the exact quantitative relationship that is to be dealt with in each new math lesson. Similarly, when you encounter new concepts or computations in your chemistry courses that require mathematical reasoning, don't hesitate to ask your chemistry teachers to review the math skills that are essential in that specific reasoning process. Many chemical concepts become meaningful only after recognizing the quantitative relationships between the number of particles involved in both the reactants and products. And it is equally impossible to understand how factors increase or decrease the rates of chemical reactions without resorting to numbers and their relationships.

One set of circumstances causes serious trouble. Sometimes there is inadequate communication between those who teach math, those who teach essential computer skills, and those who teach chemistry. Questions asked by chemistry students often become the best way for math teachers to appreciate how success in chemistry requires the ability to handle quantitative relationships. And chemistry includes many opportunities for computers to show off what they can do. There is another good solution to these communication problems. It is based on the "you teach me and I'll teach you" approach. Students who have a special knack with computers benefit from teaming up with those who grasp chemical concepts easily, and both can get a leg up from those who have no trouble with math.

COMPUTERS AND CAREERS IN CHEMISTRY

Becoming able to make computers do what you want them to do is an essential step toward chemistry-related jobs and careers. Computers have unlimited capability to store and retrieve information. They can verify each step in the mathematical derivation of even the most complex chemical concept. Data gathered during investigations can be recorded and manipulated so as to bring out the most elusive relationships among all manner of variables.

Venders of computer software offer programs that reduce the time needed to do many of the chores that come with being a chemist. The following examples include phrases from representative advertisements:

> Here is a stockroom inventory program that lets you sort and search for chemicals at the click of a mouse. Provides chemical names, formulas, and stockroom location. Stop wasting time searching through catalogs. There's no need to calculate molecular weights or find molecular formulas.

Create and analyze three-dimensional molecular structures. Generate wire-frame, ball-and-cylinder, or space-filled models. More than 50 building blocks are included in this software.

Draw chemical structures using user-friendly drawing tools. Convert chemical names to shorthand, Kekule, and structural formulas. This software allows you to change the color of any object and to move, rotate, flip and align. It recognizes trivial names, generates molecular formulas, and calculates molecular weights.

This software provides training and experience in both the theory and basics of seven of the most widely used analytical techniques, for example, chromatography, spectroscopy, radiochemistry. Includes training in making decisions while carrying out a wide range of analytical procedures.

Conduct extensive literature searches without leaving your desk. Search by author, title, abstract, or keyword. This software enables you to browse through tables of content quickly and locate items you are interested in.

This software guides you through the set-up and analysis of statistically designed experiments and offers an array of 2-D and 3-D graphs which allow you to interpret the data and communicate your findings. Special features let you focus your thoughts and energy on designing experiments instead of trudging through computer commands.

THE RISK OF BECOMING
A "COMPUTER POTATO"

Computer software promises to relieve chemists of many time-consuming chores that have kept other generations from having enough time to plan and carry out their investigations. This raises an important question. How can today's advanced computer technology give tomorrow's chemists a maximum advantage over yesterday's chemists? There is no easy answer to this question, but it is wise to keep it in mind. It is easy to become fascinated by the things computers can do. The problem seems to be keeping what they can do focused on seeking solutions to specific problems. Or, even more important, making sure their capabilities are being invested in problems of maximum importance.

When all is said and done, the real value of computer technology and its accompanying software depends upon the hypotheses that are being investigated. There is much to be gained by asking such questions as: What relationships among chemical events and circumstances will this software clarify on the way to coming up with a solution to a specific problem? What hypothesis will it help prove or disprove? Keeping questions such as these in mind is doubly productive. They bring out the valuable features of software programs and, at the same time, show how they are useful. This is somewhat like wanting to be a very good cook, to be able to prepare and serve outstanding meals. It is one thing to furnish one's kitchen with highly advanced pots and pans, gadgetry and machines, and to have a wide shelf filled with the most up-to-date cookbooks. What really matters is knowing what good food really is and how to serve it attractively.

This is like saying that becoming a successful chemist, being able to compete successfully with applicants for good jobs, depends upon knowing what chemistry really is, knowing how to do chemistry, and being aware of what chemistry can contribute to society's well-being. Computers have an almost exasperating ability to rub one's nose in procedural errors, but only the human mind can anticipate and respond to the ultimate value of any new discovery or its total impact on our society.

CHEMISTRY IN COLLEGE

Upon graduation from high school, the next step toward a career in chemistry is a two- or four-year college or university course. Although it is possible for a person to become well trained in chemistry in any one of the thousands of colleges and universities throughout the nation, the choice of a college can be difficult. Many factors, some of which are totally personal, enter into this important decision. The choice between a two- and four-year college, for example, often depends on how much money and time you are willing or able to invest before getting a job. Your choice of an institution involves your training at the high school level. You must try to determine whether you are as well trained as the students ordinarily admitted to the college or university to which you are thinking about applying.

It is doubtful that there is one best college or university for chemistry. For example, the 2,400 technically trained people employed by one large chemical industry were educated at 258 different colleges and universities. It is probably safe to say that dedicated students can gain good training in chemistry at almost any recognized college or university.

Relative expenses need not be the sole basis for choosing one college or university over another. Look into the availability of scholarships or student loans. High school or professional counselors usually know what kinds of scholarships and student loan programs are available at all colleges and universities. Consider investing more time in college and taking part-time jobs during your college years. Visits with alumni, especially alumni who majored in chemistry, can provide you with information about part-time job opportunities. Sometimes these alumni are employed in industries that provide special scholarships for young people in whom the industry is specially interested.

An amazing number of successful chemists look back on their college or university with fond and pleasant memories. It matters little whether the college was large or small, famous or obscure, richly endowed or struggling to pay expenses. It just seemed to be the right school for that particular person. It is important to feel that your choice of college or university is a good one.

When this happy state of affairs exists, invariably chemists recall very satisfactory relationships with one or more of their professors, especially those in the chemistry department. So when you are deciding on a school, what alumni have to say about their former instructors can be valuable information. Of course, individual opinions are rarely "statistically valid" samples, so each alumnus's opinion will have to be interpreted individually.

If you choose a two-year college, the program of courses in chemistry will differ somewhat from those offered during the first two years of a four-year college program. Although each college or university takes pride in its own program of courses in chemistry, there are more similarities than differences.

Most programs begin with two or three semesters of general chemistry and quantitative analysis. Students who have had high school chemistry are likely to feel that this course is a duplication of much of their high school work. In fact, some colleges and universities provide separate introductory courses for students who have and who haven't had high school chemistry. Sometimes first-year students are "sectioned" on the basis of an examination, and students with exceptionally good high school backgrounds are promoted into higher levels of the collegiate program. In all cases, the introductory courses give students a general feel for chemistry. They offer an orientation to the laboratory together with practice in some of the skills that are essential to using the laboratory effectively, an introduction to the literature of chemistry, and, of course, increased familiarity with selected principles and concepts of chemistry.

The four chemistry courses that are considered to be basic are organic, analytical, physical, and inorganic. Other courses include biochemistry, health and safety chemistry, industrial chemistry, chemical engineering, surface chemistry and catalysis, toxicology, and geochemistry. The order in which these courses are listed is based on a survey conducted by the American Chemical Society in which its members were asked to estimate the relative importance of courses that were included in their undergraduate training.

According to this survey, other worthwhile areas of undergraduate training included writing; public speaking; computer science; calculus, linear algebra, and statistics; information retrieval for chemists; physics; biology and other life sciences; and business management. Foreign languages, humanities, and social sciences were included but received less emphasis.

Organic Chemistry Courses

The introductory organic chemistry course has long been and continues to be of special concern for people who are working their way toward careers in chemistry, and particularly for those who are meeting the requirements for admission to such chemistry-related professions as medicine, dentistry, pharmacy, horticulture, and so forth. This course, although it focuses on the chemistry of a single element, acquires enormous dimensions due to the countless number of compounds in which carbon plays a role and the equally infinite importance of these compounds.

The course begins with describing the properties of the carbon atom that cause it to be involved in so many compounds. Next to be considered are compounds in which carbon combines with hydrogen. At this step in the course, students are introduced to the first necessity to establish an orderly system for naming and putting the myriad compounds of organic chemistry into orderly and manageable families. Grasping the strategy that makes this possible is the first skill that must be mastered in order to cause the organic chemistry course to be a comfortable experience.

The course unfolds by adding elements to be combined with carbon to form an ever-increasing number of compounds. As each oxygen atom is added, for example, to a molecule consisting only of carbon and hydrogen, a new family of compounds is created. And, of course, the names and properties of the members of this added family are to be learned together with the chemistry that is applied in their formation.

Although it may be difficult to believe, applying the logic that underlies the advice in these few paragraphs practically guarantees success in the introductory organic chemistry course. This is not to say, however, that organic chemistry has not become an extremely demanding branch of chemistry. Our society is constantly adding to the demands it makes on organic chemists.

The story here is well illustrated by Michael Judge in an article that appeared in the July/August 1995 issue of the *Canadian Chemical News* entitled, "Plastics in the 'Green Age': Science Fact and Fiction." It is no longer possible, for example, for chemists to concern themselves only with the coils and entanglements of polymeric molecules that give plastics the properties that make them useful; they must be concerned with such properties as biodegradability and ease of being recycled. And these properties pose special problems. For example, a plastic bottle "must somehow 'know' when it has been used and discarded, so that it doesn't fall to pieces on the supermarket shelf." Furthermore, no plastic can "vanish into nothingness. It must degrade into something, possibly exchanging one form of pollution for another."

The good news is that today's computer programs provide beautiful models of the step-by-step manner in which amazingly complex molecules can be taken apart and their fragments recombined to form new molecules. Rather than having to invest so much time in memorizing such information, today's chemists can face the challenge of designing molecules that will have the properties required to solve both today's and tomorrow's problems.

Physical Chemistry Courses

Physical chemistry is another higher level course. In this course, as the name implies, the main focus is on the role of energy transformations in the reshuffling and rearrangements of atoms from molecule to molecule. There is much emphasis on keeping track of the heat contents of reactants versus products, of the heat taken in or given off when reactions occur—in other words, the *thermodynamics* of chemical reactions. And with the heat of a reaction so closely tied in with the degree of motion of the particles in the reaction, the physical chemist deals with the *kinetics* of reactions. Thus, in the physical chemistry course, students learn to predict when collisions between molecules will or won't be followed by rearrangements of their atoms—predictions based on how rapidly the molecules were moving at the moment of impact, how much energy is needed to break existent bonds, and how much energy will be used up when new bonds form.

Higher level courses carry titles suggesting they are advanced versions of lower level courses, for example, "Advanced Organic Chemistry," or "Advanced Analytical Chemistry." Sometimes specialized courses offered for upperclass students have such titles as "Biochemistry" or "Nuclear Chemistry." Earlier training in fundamental techniques advances toward use of instruments found in industrial or research laboratories, and students become familiar with spectrophotometric, electro-analytical, and chromatographic techniques.

At the senior course level, many colleges and universities arrange to have their students enroll in courses with such titles as "Senior Research," "Individual Work for Honors," "Senior Seminar," or "Independent Study." In the spirit of these senior courses is the hope that students will develop the ability to identify problems of special interest, find their way around the literature of chemistry, and organize self-initiated and self-propelled attacks on problems.

Most four-year college and university programs do not require their students to choose a branch of chemistry in which to specialize. Students can, however, use their elective courses to concentrate their interests. The important thing, in the minds of many college counselors, is to obtain thorough knowledge of the fundamentals of chemistry, to make effective use of the laboratory, and to know how to make use of the literature of chemistry.

Graduate Programs

People differ on how far into the future they like to set the goals they want to attain. For some, one step at a time is far enough. Others like to look far ahead, even though they are not sure they have what it takes to go all of the way. Both points of view have both good and bad features. There are satisfactions in being able to achieve immediate goals. At the same time, to have a goal far into the future encourages us to take advantage of opportunities we may not have anticipated.

Setting one's sights on obtaining a master's or doctorate degree calls for planning that best begins at the four-year collegiate level. Advanced degrees require an investment of considerable time and money. By completing the proper courses at the undergraduate level, one is better able to estimate how many years will be required to earn the master's degree. Similarly, a well-planned program of courses at the master's level can include meeting all of the requirements for admission to candidacy for the doctorate degree.

It isn't easy to obtain advanced degrees in chemistry. It would be misleading to not admit that many people give up along the way. And there are several reasons why they fail to complete satisfactorily all of the requirements, particularly at the doctorate level. Primary among these reasons is being unable to maintain an acceptable life-style during the five or so years one must invest. No matter how interesting and challenging are the courses one must complete satisfactorily or how exciting is the research being done, there must be time and opportunity to take part in all of the things that make life worth living.

There are many advantages in being able to share in the camaraderie that usually prevails among graduate students. Probably even more important are pleasant relationships between graduate students and the faculty. It is to be expected that faculty members will protect the reputation of their university and, therefore, they will expect candidates for advanced degrees to measure up to traditional levels of performance. Fair play justifies letting degree candidates know what is expected from them, and that they will receive due credit for their efforts to achieve.

Know Your Adviser's Research Interests

Agreement between the research interests of faculty advisers and of the candidates they advise is a definite advantage. Many universities publish the research interests of their faculty members who sponsor graduate students. This enables degree candidates to seek sponsors whose interests are compatible with theirs. This information is usually included in publications that recruit graduate students. The following excerpts from such publications show the wide range of interests that produce options for new degree candidates:

1. Synthesis of natural products that possess potentially useful biological activity.
2. Understanding the fundamental mechanisms of diamond growth and production of thin film single crystal semiconductor diamond.
3. Emission of the so-called greenhouse gases during such biological processes as digestion in ruminates, combustion of biomass, and anaerobic decay of organic matter in rice fields.
4. Clarifying the chemical nature of intermediates in the biosynthesis of cholesterol.
5. The role of metal ions in the biological sciences and their potential use in the field of medicine.
6. Understanding the origin, mechanisms, and kinetics of mutation.

Making the Cut for Graduate Work

Being accepted for work toward advanced degrees in chemistry is by no means to be taken for granted, and this applies doubly so at universities that receive more applications than they can accept. Many graduate students receive financial assistance, which, in effect, becomes an investment on the part of the sponsoring university. And everyone is expected to protect their investments.

Factors that influence decisions to accept or reject applicants for graduate work include: grades received in undergraduate chemistry and mathematics courses, score on the Graduate Record Examination, being able to speak and write well, and recommendations by undergraduate faculty members.

It is difficult to predict how long it will take to complete the requirements for an advanced degree. There is more involved here than completing a set number of courses. Proficiency in what the required courses include must be demonstrated by passing comprehensive examinations and carrying out investigations in the laboratory. Usually a master's degree can be earned in a year or two; the doctorate in two to five or even more, particularly if the candidate combines working for the degree with part-time employment.

The Thesis Requirement

It is a long-standing tradition that the completion and defense of a research project is the culminating requirement for the doctorate degree. The research must be reported in the form of a dissertation and defended during an oral examination conducted by a committee of faculty members who are responsible for maintaining their university's scholarly standards. Meeting this requirement looms large in the minds of candidates for the doctorate degree—and rightly so. Delay in meeting this requirement is the primary cause of extending the amount of time to be invested in obtaining the degree.

Choosing the topic to be researched has much to do with producing a satisfactory dissertation. A good topic stems from the candidate's burning desire to prove or disprove a tentative explanation of a puzzling circumstance or a possible solution to a meaningful problem. It is equally important that the candidate's adviser and, ultimately, the examination committee, accept the topic as being significant. Furthermore, its investigation must be such that the candidate will show the ability to design, carry out, and report the results of experiments.

These and other features of acceptable dissertations are illustrated by an example titled, "Effects of N-3 and Trans Fatty Acids on Neonatal Survival and Brain and Liver Fatty Acids in C57BL/6 Mice." This dissertation was submitted to the faculty of the Graduate School at the University of Maryland by Julianna B. Pax. Several things sparked her interest in this topic. Other investigators had reported that diets that lacked certain kinds of fats can cause sight problems and the impairment of learning abilities. It had also been reported that Eskimos who consume large quantities of marine mammal fat have a relatively low death rate from the deposit of fatty substances in the arteries. The high death rate in the United States from fatty substances is focusing increased attention on the kinds and quantities of fats being consumed.

In the literature dealing with these observations, Dr. Pax found 189 reports of related investigations. An hypothesis of her own began taking shape. First, the effects from too much or too little of certain kinds of fats in the human diet show up first in the brain and liver tissues. Second, "good" fats differ from "bad" fats primarily in the number of carbon atoms in the long chain portion of fat molecules.

It is characteristic of doctoral research that hypotheses be sharply focused and, thereby, be manageable. On this basis, Dr. Pax limited her hypothesis to the possible effects of two fats whose molecules differ in the number of carbon atoms in the long chain portion. The basic strategy underlying her investigation consisted of feeding two groups of mice separate diets that differed only in the content of these two acids. Mice were chosen because scientists through the years have accumulated an enormous amount of information about their life processes. This information makes it possible to keep to a minimum the chances that unforeseen circumstances could affect the results from a supposedly closely controlled experiment. In addition, it is a long-standing assumption that the chemistry of digestion is the same in mice as in humans.

There were several reasons for choosing brain and liver tissues to be examined for evidence of how the two experimental diets produced different results. Brain tissue has a high fat content, but it is not easily influenced by changes in diet. Liver tissue lacks a high fat content, but it is easily influenced by changes in diet. And the liver plays a vital role in regulating the amount and kinds of fats that become available to other body organs, especially the brain.

Reporting the results from doctoral investigations poses special problems. Each result must be supported by valid data. Experimental procedures must be reproducible by other investigators. It is permitted, however, to draw implications from the data that can be shared with the public. Examples of such implications from Dr. Pax's investigation are: "Infants in poorly developed countries or from poorly nourished mothers could be at risk of survival and, if infants do survive, at risk intellectually if diets high in n-6/n-3 fatty acids are consumed by the mother and later by the child ... Infant formulas must be carefully constructed with optimum low levels of n-6/n-3 to ensure maximum brain growth and function. Pregnant mothers during the last trimester should consider eating fish at least every week."

Much satisfaction comes with being able to share such implications with other people—satisfaction that provides the motivation needed to stay with fulfilling the requirements for the doctorate degree and gaining the feeling that the final prize is really worth the effort.

Making the Most Possible from the Teaching Assistant Role

A traditional part of earning an advanced degree is helping out with the teaching duties at the university level. It is an advantage to make the most of this assignment, particularly when it includes leading discussion groups in courses taught by senior instructors. There is no better way to flesh out one's grasp of fundamental concepts and principles than by clearing up interpretations in other people's minds. Developing communication skills is a second valuable outcome from serving as a teaching assistant or research assistant, and this will propel you a notch farther up the training ladder. There are valuable things to be learned about how other people's minds work.

There are also opportunities to improve instructional methods and to develop increasingly effective teaching aids. It is to be expected that graduate students discuss the strengths and shortcomings of the instruction they are receiving during informal contacts with teaching assistants. Common sense advises against doing or saying anything that might damage human relationships, but here is an opportunity to develop interpersonal skills that may have much to do with being awarded an advanced degree and obtaining a good job after graduation.

Another Approach to Graduate Training

Canada's National Research Council is developing a type of graduate training that interlaces academic instruction with on-the-job training in the use of knowledge and know-how in solving problems on the frontier of science, particularly pharmaceuticals and the maintenance of environmental quality. This training program enables people who have experience working with the highly specialized biotechnological processes for producing new industrial products to join forces with people who have equally specialized theortical knowledge for their mutual benefit and for the benefit of the students in the program. This type of program may well point toward future opportunities for people to prepare for particularly rewarding chemistry-related careers.

CHAPTER 5

PERSONAL QUALITIES AND SUCCESS IN CHEMISTRY

One combination of character traits and human values shows up repeatedly among successful chemists. They want to produce things, to come up with what is needed to solve problems. They want to have something to show for what they have done with their time, their hands, and their minds. It does not always have to be a new kind of molecule. It may be a new or better way of doing something; or explaining something. Chemists and authors seem to be driven by similar kinds of motivations. Authors also are driven to produce things, to have something to show for their efforts. And so do artists and architects and people in many other jobs and professions.

Yes, success in chemistry comes pretty much from the same personal traits and human values that bring success in other careers. This shows through in the messages in help wanted ads for chemists. Some examples from *C & EN* are:

1. Good oral, written, and interpersonal skills.
2. Practical skills, problem solving ability, and a willingness to work in exciting team environments.

3. Utilize computer software programs to analyze equipment and statistical data, write reports, and produce diagrams and engineering drawings. Experience working with spreadsheets and graphic presentation software.
4. Work together with theoreticians in quantum, physical, and computational chemistry as well as computational biologists to attack a variety of problems.
5. Enthusiasm for laboratory work and expertise in modern techniques of synthesis, purification, and characterization.
6. Ability to write and present technical papers.
7. Ability to supervise technicians and work closely with support groups.

The personal qualities that appeal to employers are identified by J. Regis Duffy, President of Canada's Diagnostic Chemicals Limited, in "Tomorrow's Workers: An Industry Perspective." This article appeared in *Canadian Chemical News* for April 1993. "In looking at potential employees, we look for excellent reading and writing skills with a good grasp of basic chemical concepts ... who are willing to continue the learning process in a non-structured environment without any company pressure on them."

Duffy also sees enthusiasm as a wonderful trait in a prospective employee. There are enough employees whose "outlook on life is bleak." He wants employees "who have a positive, healthy outlook on life. If there are problems, one should look for solutions. If there is criticism, let it be constructive." In short, employees "need the ability to be adaptable, flexible, and motivated."

Job applicants who have had chemistry-related summer jobs or have been in co-op university industry programs have a "distinct edge." Duffy finds "these candidates have a head start in experimental procedures, and are highly motivated." From the point of view of contributing to the success of their employers, however, when all is said and done, "we appreciate employees who are able to improve a process, increase a yield, eliminate steps, decrease labor input or reduce costs."

KEEN OBSERVERS

There are certain specific qualities that are particularly evident among successful chemists. For example, chemists are experts at observation. They observe chemical events and identify a maximum number of clues about what is happening. They use their eyes, noses, and all other senses—aided when necessary, by increasingly sensitive instruments—to catch elusive bits of evidence bearing on events in the almost invisible world of interactions among molecules.

Chemists' observations tend to be made at several levels of comprehension. It isn't enough simply to observe what happens at the obvious level of flames and smoke or bubbles and precipitates. They must be able to "observe" what is happening at the totally invisible, submicroscopic level of individual atoms and molecules. Part of being good at observing chemical events is knowing what to expect. The challenge is to build mental models or images that agree with everything that can be observed. If they succeed in doing this, they can transfer what they learn by "playing with" their models to gain insight into how the particles interact. The payoff comes when chemists can control the interactions of actual atoms or molecules and cause them to do what their models led them to expect.

All chemistry begins with observation. Chemists develop this skill pretty much by remembering the things they have seen when working with similar reactions, or by recalling the observations reported by other chemists who worked with similar reactions. Chemical literature is growing so fast that one needs to be an expert in data retrieval in order to take advantage of all the observations published by fellow chemists. Nevertheless, good chemists have ready and faithful memories. Such memories enable them to retrieve past bits of information at times when they feel such information will help them understand a new situation.

Observational skill also enables one to detect important similarities or differences. The ability to recognize in seemingly different reactions one or more common observations can sometimes enable a chemist to tie together whole blocks of information. Similarly, when apparently familiar reactions bring forth an unexpectedly different observation, the alert observer can sometimes pick off a clue that can lead to a new discovery. Most important, however, is one's ability to determine whether differences or similarities are interlocked by some kind of cause-effect relationship, rather than being sheer coincidences.

Even the earliest lessons in the program of educational courses in chemistry provide opportunities to develop good observational abilities. A typical (but more than typically hazardous) school chemistry demonstration, for example, begins with dissolving a small bit of yellow phosphorus in carbon disulfide. A few drops of this solution are placed on a disc of filter paper and the filter paper is allowed to dry on top of a large graduated cylinder. After a few seconds, the paper ignites. A whistling explosion follows immediately, and the blackened filter paper disc flies from the mouth of the cylinder, leaving a whitish deposit on the walls of the cylinder.

Many students are merely startled or entertained by the unexpectedness of this noisy, smoky, smelly stunt. When the smoke and smell have cleared from the air, they think the show is over. They have had their fun and await additional entertainment. Not so with a different type of student. Assuming instructors did not tell their students everything they knew about the stunt but left it up to them to practice their own observational abilities, this second type of student probably made other subtle observations.

For instance, while the paper is drying, transparently shimmering waves can be seen sinking toward the bottom of the cylinder. Just before the noisy explosion, small yellow flames appear on the top surface of the paper disc. These flames are followed almost immediately by a slight depression or sucking in of the disc. Keen observers will see a wave of blue flame sweep down the graduated cylinder just before the much more obtrusive smoky explosion erupts upward from the cylinder. Students whose curiosity has been aroused enough to cause them to inspect the paper disc discover that the paper seems to be more discolored than charred, with streaks and blotches of yellow intermingled with black. If they examine the cylinder, they find it filled with a sharply irritating odor, and the dust on the walls leaves a yellow deposit when rubbed from the cylinder with a finger.

OBSERVATION INVITES EXPLANATION

Students who are developing the characteristics of successful chemists may be entertained by the stunt, but they are uneasy until they recognize the principles and concepts of chemistry that are involved in it. If instructors choose to play such a game, these students seem to enjoy drawing upon their own observations to put together their own explanations of the stunt—and to retrieve from past experiences the knowledge they need to interpret these observations.

For example, realizing that carbon disulfide is a volatile, high-density liquid helps one interpret the transparently shimmering waves observed sinking in the cylinder. This leads to the realization that the cylinder became filled with a mixture of carbon disulfide vapor and air while the solution was drying from the paper disc. Recalling the remarkably low kindling temperature of phosphorus, especially when finely divided, helps students understand the appearance of the yellow flames on the filter paper. Realizing that carbon disulfide is highly flammable explains the explosion of the vapor-air mixture in the cylinder.

OBSERVATION FEEDS IMAGINATION

A detailed explanation of the total stunt challenges us to move into the invisible realm of atoms and molecules. It is difficult to account for the discoloration of the disc and the whitish deposit on the walls of the cylinder without actually "seeing" molecules of carbon disulfide vapor being jostled about among the oxygen and other gas molecules in the vapor-air mixture. We must imagine their degree of motion increasing abruptly at the moment the phosphorus catches fire on the paper disc. Under the greatly increased motion, the impact of collisions between the molecules of the vapor-air mixture would be enhanced greatly. Bonds holding the molecules of carbon disulfide intact would be broken, liberating free atoms of carbon and sulfur. The bonds holding the atoms together in oxygen molecules will also break. In the chaotic collisions among these fractured molecules, new arrangements of the fragments forming new bonds would surely occur. It is logical to "see" new molecules of carbon dioxide and sulfur dioxide forming. And if the energy of these newly formed products is less than was present in the original reactants, the excess energy can be assumed to raise the temperature of all of the gases in the system with explosively rapid expansion.

If so inclined, we can carry our explanation of the stunt on and on. And curious students do. They may "see" a larger number of carbon disulfide molecules being fractured in the chaotic collision environment than there are molecules of oxygen. This leads to the deposit of free carbon or free sulfur on exposed surfaces, explaining the discoloration of the paper disc and the deposit on the wall of the cylinder. But why wasn't the paper charred or set on fire? Perhaps, we argue, the temperature of the exploding gases and the burning phosphorus during the moment of their existence simply did not raise the temperature of the paper to its kindling temperature, and the swooshing gases blew out the initial flames.

What we are trying to do here is describe what goes on in the mind of a person who is figuring out an explanation of something unexplained. We are contemplating the highly mysterious activities that go on in people's minds. The human brain has been claimed to have enormous abilities to receive, store, and process data. There is a degree of logic in saying that success in chemistry hinges on such abilities—abilities some people claim you are either born with or without. Other people believe these abilities can be developed and exercised. The important thing is that you should enjoy the exercise.

This phosphorus-carbon disulfide stunt sometimes brings out another feature of what it takes to be a good observer. Sometimes students have seen the stunt and had it explained to them without going very far into the whole chemistry of the reactions. Thus, they feel they will be able to explain the stunt without exercising their full powers of observation. What can be even more dangerous, they may ignore observations and simply not see anything that would conflict with a satisfactory explanation.

In the spirit of the old proverb, "none are so blind as those that will not see," it is so easy to overlook things, or to close our minds to observations that don't seem to fit in with the way we have already decided something should be. For example, the next time you have an opportunity to observe the phosphorus-carbon disulfide stunt, notice how easy it is to ignore the momentary depression or sucking in of the filter paper disc. Think how seriously such behavior could handicap a chemist who wants to understand fully what is really happening during a chemical event.

IMAGINATION AND INVENTIVENESS

Chemists tend to have good imaginations, inventiveness, and creativity. It isn't enough simply to pack one's mind with observations and related data from wherever they can be gathered. Successful chemists must be able to put all such raw material together and come up with more than they had to start with. The ability we are talking about here is a strange blend of hunch, intuition, insight, and inference. It also contains a dash of courage, especially if the new idea contradicts established points of view or opens up a totally new way of looking at something. The history of chemistry tells of many situations in which a man or woman who came up with a new idea was made to feel very, very lonesome by established chemists. Fortunately, history seems to favor the rebel more often than the people who turn cold shoulders.

Chemists don't give up easily. Theirs is a kind of bulldog persistence, blended with the boxer's clever maneuvering for a better position from which to attack. They are patient in an impatient sort of way. They launch research or development projects that they know will take years to pull off before final results are in. But they may show impatience while waiting for a pot to boil or a solid to dissolve. It is as though they are willing to wait for long-term results but insist on knowing that they are doing everything as promptly as possible toward moving their projects forward.

Chemists must learn to live with frustration, disappointment, and failure: the plastic that persists in being too brittle, the drug with bad side effects, the catalyst that contaminates rather than enhances the yield from a reaction. A research laboratory director once said that his most soul-searching decisions are those he must make when the time comes to pull a team off a project. There is always the haunting feeling that success might break through if additional resources are committed to the project—a feeling likely to be deeply felt by the men and women who have already invested time in the project. But there is also the possibility that these people would achieve equally satisfying successes much sooner if they were reassigned to new projects.

Successful chemists seem to enjoy intellectual exchange with their co-workers. At the same time, it is easy for them, when needed, to slip away to a quiet place to incubate ideas or give their imaginations free rein. Successful chemists can take in stride the long stretches of time when breakthroughs simply won't come and still have faith that, sooner or later, they will.

CHAPTER 6

CAREER SPECIALTIES IN CHEMISTRY

Chemists like to think of themselves as practicing their profession in one of several fields. *Analytical chemists* specialize in determining the composition of substances. They are the "what" and "how much" chemists. *Inorganic chemists* are ready to deal with taking apart or putting together all molecules except those whose properties are primarily due to containing carbon. Compounds that contain carbon as the most significant element are of special interest to *organic chemists. Biochemists,* in turn, are ready to tackle the chemistry of any compound that is a part of the living world. The role energy plays in chemical reactions is of special interest to *physical chemists.*

SPECIALIZATION CAN BE MISLEADING

The idea of specialization can be misleading when viewed from the perspective of being well prepared to seek employment. This applies both to jobs on university campuses and in the chemical industry. For example, a "positions available" notice in *Chemical and Engineering News (C & EN),* is headlined, "Analytical Chemistry," but the job description reads, "The successful candidate will be expected to teach courses at all levels of our ACS certified chemistry program, develop a vigorous undergraduate research program, and contribute to the all-college interdisciplinary liberal studies curriculum."

In this same publication, notices of positions that are available in industrial chemistry carry such headlines as: materials scientist, environmental chemist, pesticide residue chemist, medicinal chemist, polymer chemist, bioanalytical chemist, and process engineer.

The confusion here seems to come from administrative practices that require specifying a limited number of employment opportunities or slots to be filled. The first thing applicants need to do is to show they have the credentials required to fill a slot. For example, if a position-open announcement specifies an analytical chemist, it is an advantage for job applicants to be able to identify themselves as analytical chemists, even though the job description calls for competency in other areas. The point to be made here is that although an applicant thinks of herself or himself as, say, an environmental chemist, there can be advantages in being prepared to qualify for one of the more traditional chemistry specialties.

To continue this confusing state of affairs, many employers want their new people to be well trained in a basic field and, at the same time, have the training that gives them a head start when they are assigned to a specific problem. One way to meet this situation is to concentrate on the same topic or bit of chemistry each time a term paper is assigned or when there are opportunities for independent study or research.

CHEMISTRY TEACHERS

The satisfactions that come with chemistry-related jobs and careers are to be found in classrooms, lecture halls, and teaching laboratories. These opportunities are not only available in all communities, they yield the satisfactions that are to be gained by practicing two professions. Furthermore, there is a certain catalytic effect that comes with combining both the teaching and practicing of chemistry. To be in an environment where people are discovering things for the first time is almost as stimulating as being in one's own laboratory and discovering something that no one ever knew before. Yes, it is second-hand or vicarious satisfaction, but there are advantages in knowing that this satisfaction can be experienced regularly as opposed to the rare chance that it will occur in a research laboratory.

Sometimes chemists enjoy great satisfactions by launching into the unknown simply to see what is out there. Similar satisfactions await teachers when they take their students on this kind of excursion.

There is a bad news side to all of this. Teachers must deal with attitude problems. Not always do their students come with open minds about who chemists are and what they do. The popular news media's treatment of society's problems can leave chemists being seen as the cause even when they are actually looking for solutions, particularly when the actual causes could not have been anticipated. There is another kind of public image problem. An example is the proclaimed superiority of "natural" or "organic" foods over those produced by established agricultural and food preparation practices that rely on the use of products from the chemical industry.

Chemistry teachers can exercise their investigative and creative talents by seeking better ways to nurture the learning process. This area of research can be uniquely rewarding. It has been known that learning is difficult to come by. Teachers have the right to take pride in inventing new ways to nudge students toward discovering for themselves a chemical concept, law, or principle—this being the kind of cerebral exercise that best nurtures effective learning.

In many respects, success in the chemistry classroom depends upon personal attributes that resemble those that bring success in the chemistry research laboratory. Glenn T. Seaborg touched on this several years ago when he talked to the young men and women who were taking part in the 14th National Science Fair International in Albuquerque, New Mexico. Dr. Seaborg, a Nobel laureate, knew that his audience included the kind of young people upon whom the future of chemistry depends:

> "Creative research calls for a combination of qualities, only one of which is superior intelligence. It is difficult to specify the combination of characteristics which may be of crucial importance for success in solving a specific scientific problem. Perhaps an intuition or a 'feel' derived from lengthy experience with certain types of phenomena, perhaps special knowledge of a new instrumental technique, perhaps a natural manual dexterity in some important type of laboratory manipulation, perhaps an unreasonable stubbornness in seeking a better explanation of some phenomenon which others have passed by as 'explained' may be the key to a fruitful series of developments . . . Maybe it's just plain hard work, because, without

downright hard work, there can be no success in a scientific career."

THE ORGANIC CHEMIST

While the twentieth century was winding down, several things happened that brought the organic chemists to the forefront of the chemistry enterprise. Rather than continuing to rely on petroleum for the primary source of their raw materials, research chemists "discovered" that living systems can do far more than provide the molecules that are to yield the fragments to be reassembled to form new and more useful molecules. It was realized that the chemistry of living systems can be not only described accurately, but managed even to the point of scaling up to produce commercial quantities of molecules that are so complex that they could not be produced profitably by the usual methods of chemical synthesis.

Here is one of many possible examples. The drag-line silk of the orb-weaving spider is very strong and stretches considerably before it breaks. These are ideal properties for a textile fiber. But who imagines using enough spiders to spin commercial quantities of fiber? Nonetheless it is feasible to transfer the spider's gene that codes for the fiber's molecule to a bacteria that can be cultured in unlimited quantities and at an adequately low cost.

Polyphenylene is another interesting example. This polymer is uniquely valuable because it can be converted to a semiconductor. When first developed, it was synthesized by coupling the oxidation of benzene with the reduction of cupric chloride in the presence of aluminum chloride. Recently, a strain of bacteria was discovered in a waste dump that had been contaminated with hydrocarbons for many years. This bacteria will oxidize benzene to form an intermediate molecule that readily becomes polyphenylene. To suggest the potentialities of this way to solve synthesis problems, the name of this molecule is 5,6-*cis*-dihydroxycyclohexa-1,3-diene.

PLAYING GAMES WITH NATURE'S CHEMISTRY

There's more here than simply duplicating nature's chemistry. There is the appreciation of how chemistry solves the fantastic array of problems that make life what it is in its myriad forms. When all is taken into account, no matter where life occurs, from Arctic ice fields to undersea volcanic vents, somehow the necessary combinations of atoms are brought together to produce molecules that have the properties that enable one or another species to survive. Modern research tells us that all chemistries are manageable. This brings the challenge to go nature one better. We are not to accept sickness or hunger, discomfort or despair, or any other personal or social problem simply as something to put up with. If there are no limits to the kinds of problems other species solve, chemistry certainly holds unlimited promise of doing its part to solve humanity's problems.

Progress is being made, and necessary governmental regulations are being worked out. Already efforts to produce antibiotics, hormones, vaccines, and antibodies are under way. Redesigned bacteria do a better job of getting rid of wastes. Plants that are resistant to herbicides and insecticides, tomatoes that ripen better, fish that grow faster, and farm crops that can be processed more efficiently, too, are being developed.

THE ANALYTICAL CHEMIST

Several things are happening that increase the number of job opportunities for analytical chemists. New government regulations require labels that give more information about the nutrient value of foods. And the medical professions are relying more and more on analytical chemists to help them to diagnose diseases and dysfunctions. At the same time, thanks to automated instruments such as sequential multiple analyzers, table-top analyzers, and "dipstick" procedures, many analytical chores can be accomplished quickly by people with only a minimum of specialized training.

Actually, there is much more to being an analytical chemist than matching colors or reporting the readout from printers. Although well-trained technicians can master these skills, someone must understand the fundamental chemistry that makes analytical tests possible and how that chemistry relates to the health or industrial processes for which the analyses are being carried out.

Plants That Reverse Pollution

The role of analytical chemistry is well illustrated in a research project that takes advantage of the ability of some kinds of plants to remove pollutants from the soil, particularly soils that have been contaminated with cadmium or zinc, and with less success, lead, nickel, uranium, and cobalt. A fundamental step depended upon being able to prove that certain kinds of plants absorb one or more of these metals from the soil, and that the absorbed metal is retained in the leaves or stem. This step also included determining how much of the polluting metal was in any soil sample.

Analytical chemistry is a part of the training that has enabled Rufus Chaney, an agronomist at the U.S. Department of Agriculture's Environmental Chemistry Laboratory, to head up a team to do this research. After locating areas near smelter and mining sites, waste dumps, and landfills that were known to be heavily polluted with these metals, the next step was to determine the kinds of plants that could survive in such environments. The research team gained an assist here from prospectors who know that certain kinds of plants yield clues to the presence of metallic ore deposits.

The Alpine pennycress came to take first place in the ability to absorb zinc from contaminated soils. In fact, an acre of this rather unpretentious weed can remove and store more than 100 pounds of zinc during a growing season. To add to the appeal of this solution to a pollution problem, the market value of this much zinc promises to make this decontamination procedure self-supporting.

To add to the role of analytical chemistry in this research project, blood and urine analyses of residents in areas contaminated with zinc and cadmium yielded valuable information about whether grains, fruits, and vegetables grown in contaminated soils affect the amount of these metals in body tissues.

The work of other scientists who are joining in this research effort illustrates another feature of analytical chemistry that is gaining in importance. This work seeks to identify the specific gene or genes that enable pennycress to be so effective in storing zinc. If this goal is attained, the next step will be to transfer these genes to plants that are easy to grow and harvest high yields.

Lab Tests from Another Point of View

The scope and importance of analytical chemistry was beautifully illustrated several years ago when the Apollo 11 mission returned with its sample of moon rocks. Plans for this very special event began years before the rocket was launched. The total team of analytical chemists consisted of nearly 150 principal investigators from the United States, Canada, Finland, Belgium, England, Germany, Switzerland, Japan, and Australia. For more than three years, the United States spent some $4 million annually to outfit laboratories and organize the assignments for the members of the team.

The decision was made to turn over 85 percent of the returned samples to this team. Of the remaining samples, 10 percent were to be used for biological and quarantine testing and 5 percent were to be saved for permanent displays and exhibitions.

Plans called for covering four major investigative areas. Thirty-four of the team members were to describe the samples from the point of view of mineralogy and petrology. This part of the total plan ensured that the mineral content of the rock samples would be determined and all peculiarities of crystal structure carefully observed. The petrologists were to gather all of the clues they could in order to describe the origin and history of the rocks.

The chemical and isotopic analysis of the rocks was the responsibility of 56 of the people on the team. These chemists were to determine not only the kinds and numbers of atoms in the molecules or crystal units of which the rocks are composed, but also to specify which isotopes of each element are present. The physical properties of the rocks were the responsibility of 33 of the chemists, and the remaining 19 were responsible for the biological or biochemical and organic analyses.

To read about the individual assignments of these 150 analytical chemists brings to mind the great differences between the way modern chemistry handles the "what and how much" questions and the way analyses were carried out a few years ago. It is easy to imagine an old prospector, even today, picking samples of potentially rich ores from a mountainside pretty much as the astronauts would probably heft the moon rocks, crack several together to estimate hardness, and try to recognize similarities to other kinds of rocks or minerals with which they were already familiar.

The old prospector might very well carry in the field an alcohol lamp, a lump of charcoal, and a blowpipe—and he would use these tools to see if the ore sample showed certain properties when subjected to a hot, pointed flame on a bed of hot carbon. Or he might toss a few grains of the ore into his campfire to see if the flames turned colors, as he had learned to associate with certain kinds of ores or minerals. Note what the prospector is doing to analyze his ore samples. He is simply subjecting the unknown materials to certain tests or reactions. If the reactions produce certain observable results, he knows those results are very likely to occur only when certain elements or minerals exist in his rock samples.

Each of the 150 analytical chemists employed basically the same sort of strategy in answering their assigned questions about the composition of the moon rocks. But the nature of their assignments show the advancement that has taken place in the science and art of analytical chemistry. Here are some representative assignments: Determine fourteen elements by neutron activation analysis. Measure cosmic ray-induced ^{26}Al content. Determine mass spectrometric analyses for organic matter in lunar crust. Measure natural and induced thermoluminescence to determine history and environmental features of lunar materials. Determine crystal structures of sulfide and related minerals. Study the texture, composition, and relationship of minerals. Using Mossbauer and nuclearmagnetic resonance techniques, measure the oxidation states of iron, radiation damage, and Al, Na, and Fe energy state in crystals. Perform elemental analysis and mineral phase studies by electron microprobe. Identify organic compounds in lunar material by means of gas chromatography-mass spectrometry, NMR, high-speed liquid chromatography, and variations on these techniques.

The Strategy of Analysis

Many of these assignments carry overwhelming terms. To chemists who have been trained in the use of the required instruments and who understand the scientific principles upon which the instruments operate, however, these analytical techniques are just as simple as the prospector's blowpipe analyses are to the prospector. In the case of neutron activation analysis, for example, the chemist using this technique understands that each kind of atom is characterized by having a set number of protons and neutrons per nucleus. If additional neutrons are fired into the nuclei of the atoms of one kind of element and an unstable isotope of that element is produced, sooner or later a fragment will be ejected from the nuclei. The characteristics of the ejected fragment can be identified. Each kind of radioactive nucleus ejects fragments unique in terms of half-life and energy characteristics. Thus, when a certain kind of fragment is ejected from an atom that was made radioactive by having a neutron fired into its nucleus, the chemist can deduce what kind of atom was the original target hit by the neutron.

Comparable techniques are used with electron microprobes, mass spectrometers, and laser microprobes. Each of these analytical techniques enables the analyst to compare the interaction of "unknown" elements with a carefully controlled energy probe against the interaction of this same energy probe with known elements. In the hands of a well-trained chemist, exceedingly tiny samples of material can be analyzed with parts per million precision.

Chemists develop easily done tests for elements or compounds that must be repeated many times. For example, the presence of sugar in urine can be quantitatively estimated simply by observing color changes in specially prepared paper. At a more sophisticated level, substances can be analyzed by taking advantage of the uniqueness with which each substance allows different wavelengths of light to pass through. By using a spectrophotometer to measure the amount of light being absorbed by the substance being analyzed and by constantly changing the wavelength of the light, the analyst obtains evidence of the kinds of atom-to-atom bonds that hold the molecules of the unknown substance together. The graphic record of the substance's absorption or transmission of a range of different wavelengths produces a very effective "fingerprint" whereby the substance can be identified.

Less complex equipment and simpler principles are involved in chromatographic analytical methods. In fact, some very difficult analysis problems are solved very effectively using only strips of ordinary filter paper or thin layers of chalky substances spread on sheets of glass or clear plastic. Underlying chromatographic analytical procedures is the assumption that each kind of molecule being jostled through a nonmoving substance by the action of a moving solvent will move at a unique rate. Squeeze the juice from flower petals, for example, and place a tiny drop of these squeezings at the bottom of a strip of filter paper. The cellulose fibers of the paper are the nonmoving medium. Hang the filter paper strip so that the bottom edge touches a liquid that is likely to dissolve the flower petal pigments responsible for the color of the flower. As the solvent moves up the strip by capillary action, each separate pigment from the flower petal will be swept or jostled along at its own rate. By the time the solvent reaches the top of the filter paper strip, hopefully, each separate pigment will occupy separate spots marking where it was moved by the advancing solvent. Pigments not at all soluble in the chosen solvent, of course, will remain in the original spot, but this simple process enables the analytical chemist to find out what kinds of pigments are blended together to produce the colors of many kinds of flowers.

The literature of chemistry contains many reports of solvents that work well in specific chromatographic analyses and the rates at which various kinds of substances are moved by each solvent. A special type of chromatography separates mixtures of gases by allowing them to diffuse or be swept through long tubes or columns packed with a nonmoving solid. As with other types of chromatography, each kind of gas molecule diffuses or is swept along at a unique rate.

Identifying substances by taking advantage of their unique interactions with a moving phase is developing rapidly. This analytical strategy is being improved constantly by discovering more efficient solvents or more sensitive methods for detecting the separated substances. Already very complex substances that exist in amazingly low concentrations are being identified.

INORGANIC CHEMISTRY

Although there are many more chemists specializing in the chemistry of carbon and its compounds than there are specializing in all of the remaining elements, inorganic chemists are an equally essential group within the total chemical endeavor. Their importance can be judged by thinking about some of the special fields of inorganic chemistry.

A few years ago, among 6,700 inorganic chemists, 900 were specializing in the chemistry of coordination compounds, a class of substances in which the particle units are much more complex than the usual inorganic compound's molecules. These complex particles occur sometimes during halfway steps during a chemical reaction, especially after the reactants have been dissolved or melted. In order to describe the reaction with sufficient precision to manage or control the reaction and make it do what the chemist wants, he or she needs to understand the structure of these intermediate particles as well as the beginning and end reactants and products.

Molecules with Unique "Assignments"

Sometimes a reaction can be controlled by deliberately introducing some kind of "complexing" agent into the reaction. For example, suppose a physician decides that a patient's disease can be cured no other way than by giving the patient a dose of a medicine that contains an element that, if the total molecule were taken apart, would be quite toxic. In other words, although the total medicine might cure the patient, the residues from the medicine left in the patient's blood stream might make the patient sicker after than before the treatment. By taking advantage of coordination compound chemistry, a second substance could be included in the medicine that would "complex" or tie up the newly released dangerous elements in complex molecules or ions that would be thrown off in body wastes before causing any damage.

These complexing agents have descriptive names. Some are called *clathrates,* a name derived from the cagelike structure of their molecules. Other particles become "trapped" in the cage structures of the complexing agent molecule and are thus kept from interfering with a reaction, even though it is impossible to remove them from the total reaction system. Another possibility is that the clathrate molecule would be made to "cage" a particle during the early steps of a reaction and, when the appropriate intermediate step comes up, a new reactant would be introduced that would break down the "cage walls" and release the trapped particles so they can play the required role in the complex reaction. A third type of complexing agent has molecules with groups of atoms that reach out, so to speak, and grab certain kinds or sizes of other particles with which they come into contact. These are the *chelating agents,* a name derived from a Greek word meaning *claw.*

Many inorganic chemists devote their time to synthesizing new compounds, especially new compounds needed for putting into general use the new inventions of their colleagues in chemical engineering and technology. Today, for example, many synthesis specialists put top priority on materials for transistors and other solid-state materials for the electronics industry. A close second, however, is work with the boron and silicon compounds. This fact suggests that the very old industries built around clay, glass, asbestos, and related materials continue to provide employment opportunities for inorganic chemists.

Many inorganic chemists prefer to identify a fundamental chemical principle or concept as their special field. We find chemists specializing in the equilibrium and thermodynamic relationships in inorganic reactions, inorganic polymers, or solutions and the theory of solvents. Chemists specializing in the first of these areas become experts on those reactions that produce products that are sufficiently similar to the original reactants that the reaction "reverses" itself, so to speak, and both reactants and products coexist in the reacting vessel. Polymer specialists become experts on those small molecules that can be made to hook to each other in chain fashion to produce very large units with new and, sometimes, very useful properties.

PHYSICAL CHEMISTRY

As the name implies, physical chemists keep one eye on the atoms and molecules in reactions and the other eye on the energy transformations. The invisibility of both atoms and energy allows this metaphor to emphasize how much physical chemists deal with models—usually mathematical and always mental. Yet there are very real bridges between the mathematically derived descriptions of the route a reaction will follow, as conceived in the mind of a physical chemist, and the route the reaction actually follows in the plumbing of an industrial version of the reaction.

Electrochemistry, followed closely by *catalysis* and *surface chemistry,* is the specialty of physical chemistry with which the greatest numbers of chemists identify themselves. Electrical energy transformations, whether they occur in the storage battery of an automobile or in the ghostly colored light show of the aurora borealis, produce significant changes in the properties of matter. Conversely, when chemical changes in matter are accompanied by recoverable quantities of electrical energy—quantities of energy adequate, perhaps, to drive our automobiles or fly planes without flooding the atmosphere with noxious gases—physical chemists will find themselves involved in highly important social and economic problems.

Chemical reactions that are influenced by light, as in photographic processes, or that produce light as an accompanying event, fall into the domain of physical chemists. And it matters not whether these reactions occur in the flashing firefly or in the newly developed glass for the windshields of aircraft that, when subjected to bright sunlight, discolors to provide an automatic sunshield. Obviously, this glass retrieves its colorless transparency in the absence of bright sunlight.

A national directory lists 300 chemists specializing in flames and explosives, 400 in high-temperature chemistry, and 700 in thermochemistry and thermodynamics. Another 1,200 chemists identify themselves as experts in one or another of the phase changes that occur when the temperature of substances change sufficiently to cause the substances to freeze or melt, evaporate or condense.

Polymerization chemistry attracts many physical chemists. In many polymers, spectacular changes occur when the small unit particles, the monomer, join to form large units, the polymer. Ethylene, for example, is a colorless gas. Polyethylene, on the other hand, can be a very substantial material from which we make many useful items. These changes in properties that accompany the polymerization of polyethylene fall in the domain of the physical chemist.

At one time, 500 physical chemists stated their specialty to be nuclear and radiochemistry, 400 radiation and hot-atom chemistry, and another 100 isotope effects. These data indicate that energy transformations occurring within the nuclei of atoms, usually the domain of "pure" physicists, can be the special interests of physical chemists. With society's demands for ever-increasing quantities of available energy against an ever-decreasing store of fossil fuels in the form of coal and petroleum, we may predict that opportunities will expand for employment in the research laboratories and industrial organizations whose interests involve nuclear energy.

THE FIELDS OF CHEMISTRY
FROM ANOTHER POINT OF VIEW

A good answer to the question—What kind of chemist are you setting out to be?—depends on the situation in which the question is being asked. If the question is asked as "small talk" among chemists who are becoming acquainted with each other, it is good to be able to say that you are one of the well-established varieties of chemist. Invariably, however, further conversation brings out that most chemists prefer to be identified as being a specialist in enzymes, DNA, semiconductors, polymers, or almost any other specialty.

It is almost a matter of gamesmanship to be able to identify oneself with a currently significant special field or "in" problem and, at the same time, let it be known that you are well trained in one of the four or five basic branches of chemistry. It is usually an advantage to be identified early as having majored in a basic field and then allow the conversation to move toward a topic in which you have acquired special training or experience.

Another awkward question is: Are you in "pure" or "applied" chemistry? This question is awkward because, in one sense, all projects in chemistry lead to description and, hence, to management, control, or use. The immediate goal of a chemist may be simply to describe or explain what is going on in a reaction. But there is no telling when this chemist or someone else will begin thinking about putting the description to use in one way or another.

Chemists, for example, may spend many hours investigating the oxygen transfer across the human placenta, from the mother's blood to the developing tissues of her unborn baby. They find that the total process is affected by the rate of blood flow through the capillaries, the oxygen content and tension of capillary blood, pH, the rate of release of oxyhemoglobin, and so forth. Information such as this is the goal of their research, but it is difficult to imagine that the chemists don't at least hope that somewhere, some day, some mother's baby will have a better start toward a healthy life because they discovered this knowledge.

Other chemists may discover that the sex life of a male cotton boll weevil involves the compound, 2-isopropenyl-1-methyl-cyclobutaneethanol. "So what?" asks the nonchemist. But what the nonchemist doesn't know is that if chemists were able to synthesize this exotic compound and make it available in commercial quantities, the compound could well protect fields of cotton from a very expensive pest without polluting the countryside with a more toxic insecticide.

When most people drive by a sewage disposal plant, they simply wrinkle their noses and complain about the bad smells. But chemists may begin wondering why the reactions that produce the bad smells cannot be brought under control. Rather than tossing the sewage high into the air in the hope that atmospheric oxygen will "purify" it, the chemists may decide to look into the idea of pumping liquid oxygen directly into the sewage in closed tanks. In this case, they may launch an investigation generated directly by an urge to solve a social problem, but at the same time they will still be looking for basic, fundamental knowledge.

Chemists caught in traffic behind motor buses belching vile-smelling exhaust gases may decide that there are no good reasons why motor fuels cannot be refined sufficiently to produce only water and carbon dioxide when burned. But they may also realize that they will have to team up with social, political, and economic scientists in order to accomplish what they have in mind. And they may need the help of engineers, mechanical as well as chemical, to prove that their ideas are practical. In this case, the chemists' success doesn't depend so much on their chemical specialties as it does on their ability to work with people, not only in many branches of chemistry but in other human endeavors, as well.

As is true with many professions, chemists can choose between knowing something about many kinds of reactions, and knowing everything possible about only a very few reactions. There are strengths and weaknesses in both choices. The nonspecialists must be ready to work with people who know more about the problem at hand than they themselves do. The extreme specialists run the risk of having their specialties become obsolete or of being done in by a problem that they might have solved with wider training and experience.

It is difficult to predict trends in the specific demand for specially trained chemists in industrial organizations, hospitals, research centers, and the other places where chemists are employed. In general, how wise it is to put "all of one's eggs in a very small basket" depends upon how widely applicable are the principles and concepts of chemistry that underlie the special area of interest.

CAREERS CLOSELY RELATED TO CHEMISTRY

No clear-cut boundaries separate careers in chemistry from many careers in special fields of physics, biology, and geology. On this basis, a person can shift career interests from one field to another without undue sacrifice of the time and money invested in training pointed originally toward a career in chemistry. In addition to physics, biology, and geology, training in chemistry can also be redirected toward careers in medicine, dentistry, pharmacy, and other kinds of employment in the health field. The work in these fields is being approached increasingly from the molecular level. And, in many ways, the discipline and work habits needed for success in chemistry parallel rather closely the requirements for success in these related fields.

When chemists shift to other branches of science, the dimensions of their problems may change. In geology, for example, rather than working with beaker- or flask-size samples of substances, they may confront mountain-size ore bodies or rock strata. In biology, the few grams of a substance chemists may have studied in a test tube may now be distributed throughout the body tissues of a two-ton elephant. In practice, it seems to be easier for chemists to scale up their perspectives and study phenomena on a large scale than it is for scientists without training in chemistry to learn how to shift their perspectives from looking at phenomena, in a general sort of way, to looking for the atom-molecular origins of these phenomena.

Chemists can shift to other lines of work without actually leaving the total endeavor of chemistry. Many chemistry-based industries use sales reps and business executives for whom a background in chemistry is either a necessity or a very great advantage. On this basis, men and women who decide that they were not cut out to be "test tube" chemists can stay close to their original career interest and still enjoy satisfactions from almost totally different careers.

The rapid evolution of many aspects of our society creates needs for technically capable people, under circumstances that often do not allow colleges and universities time to develop training programs that produce graduates with the required capabilities. Nuclear science, for example, rapidly developed a program of research and technology calling for many scientists and technicians having highly specialized capabilities. These needs developed more rapidly than universities could develop adequate training programs to turn out a new generation of nuclear scientists. In retrospect, many people who were well trained in basic chemistry redirected their careers and gained the knowledge and skills they needed to work as nuclear scientists. Their success demonstrates that training in chemistry can be exploited when new challenges and opportunities arise in other branches of science.

Recent but rapidly expanding developments in biogenetics provide career opportunities that require knowledge and know-how that can come only by blending chemistry with other professions. These opportunities begin with understanding chemical processes as they occur in one or another life form. A second step is to identify the genes that control these processes. At this point, chemists must team up with people in the life sciences in order to solve the problems that arise in connection with using these chemical processes not so much to serve the needs of other living systems, but to serve humanity's needs.

The satisfactions to be gained from such efforts are tremendous; so are the responsibilities. A basic step is to reshuffle genes from one species to another—from one species in which the desired chemical process occurs but under noneconomic conditions, to a species in which the same chemistry can occur but under such conditions that make possible the production of economically profitable quantities. At the responsibilities level, there is no way to predict how the introduction of alien genes into "workhorse" species will affect the lifestyle of that species and how it interacts with other species including, of course, mankind.

CHAPTER 7

SECURING EMPLOYMENT

Let's begin with some general good advice. Finding a job boils down to two sets of circumstances: one, somebody needs someone to do something, and two, you must prove that you are that someone. Furthermore, your potential employer will want to know that you will be reliable, easy to work with in your present job, and anxious to earn promotion.

Now for more advice but of a slightly different kind. It involves the often repeated notion, "It isn't what you know, it's who you know." Whether this works to your advantage depends upon how you use it. The more you know about what a potential employer's needs are, the easier it is to convince him or her to hire you. And friends usually supply this kind of information. Similarly, friends usually rely on each other for information about the personal qualifications of new employees.

As pointed out earlier, the good news is that chemistry enables young people to get a head start in enjoying being a part of a widely recognized profession. Nor are entry-level jobs destined to be dead-end jobs. Experience on the job can be enough to earn advancement. In many communities, however, employers encourage their employees to enroll in college-level chemistry courses evenings or weekends while they are holding down full-time jobs.

FROM THE EMPLOYER'S POINT OF VIEW

What we are saying here can be fleshed out by citing descriptions of jobs to be filled by the personnel department of a large corporation that develops and distributes the chemicals and equipment needed to make adequate supplies of safe water available to customers. The following citations give the position title, job grade, job prerequisites, educational requirements, experience requirements, position summary, and representative duties performed. It is to be particularly noted that job grade levels rise as education and experience increases. In effect, this becomes a ladder that allows one to see how far into the chemistry profession to set goals, and what it will take to get there.

Analytical Technician II: High school diploma, math/science aptitude. No previous training is required. On-the-job training will be provided. Performs sample preparations, routine physical and chemical analysis. Performs filtrations, digestions, grindings, dilutions. Runs the following analyses: pH, conductance, titrations, solids. Disposes of samples. Washes glassware. Prepares new corrosion test specimens. Performs other work related duties as assigned.

Research Technician II: High school and some college course work. Accurate typing at 50 wpm and demonstrated laboratory skills. Performs clerical duties for the library 60% of the time and supports the laboratory by performing screening tests, etc., during 40% of work time. Performs regular duties, including typing, filing, photocopying, maintenance of circulation records, circulation of library materials, and ordering patents. Prepares testing and treating solutions and calibration standards for screening function. Conducts routine screening tests (Ca^2+ ion sensitivity and complexition). Maintains laboratory (cleans glassware and work area). Assists in chemical inventory maintenance. Maintains safe work area.

Analytical Research Technician I: High school plus one year college chemistry. Two years related experience. Performs routine technical operations with minimum supervision. Conducts assigned experiments; observes, records, and reports results under the supervision of group leader or higher level scientist. Performs routine maintenance of equipment and laboratory. Performs other duties as assigned.

Senior Field Test Services Technician: College chemistry. Formulating and/or chemical laboratory experience is essential. Formulates all chemical reagents and solutions in accordance with specifications and ensures all quality control standards are met regarding product. Maintains statistical records relating to formulations and quality control analysis; consults with laboratory technical personnel when necessary. Maintains adequate levels of raw materials and ensures proper stocking and operation of laboratory equipment and apparatus. Performs and documents the receiving of inbound materials as to order content and accuracy and verifies/recommends the payment of vendor invoices pertaining thereto.

Research Technician I: High school diploma, two semesters college chemistry, associate degree preferred. Mechanical aptitude. Conducts experiments under the guidance of a senior scientist. Observes, records, and presents in written and oral form the results of experiments completed. Contributes activity toward the development of experimental procedures. Participates in development of technical expertise in assigned areas of responsibility. Maintains the laboratory equipment and supplies. Conducts analyses of field samples as required.

Analytical Research Assistant II: High school diploma, math/science aptitude, one year related experience. Answers and redirects, when appropriate, all incoming telephone calls to the department. Transmits results of analytical reports to clients when appropriate. Processes additions and modifications to the analytical procedure database. Maintains the competitive treatment database files. Plans, performs, observes, and records the results of routine analyses, under the direction of an analytical supervisor. Makes suggestions for the improvement of assigned projects and assists in the development of new procedures.

Research Scientist II: B.S. in biochemistry. Working knowledge of chemistry; microbiological research experience. Designs and conducts research and development experiments requiring a good understanding of general knowledge of chemistry. Responsibilities include one major and/or other smaller projects or parts of other larger projects. Works independently with management guidelines. Conducts assigned experiments in chemistry. Observes, records, analyzes, and interprets findings. Develops experimental formulations and methods of analyzing their performance. Prepares data summary on findings in written and formal format. Communicates with co-workers and management in the reporting and/or discussion of findings. Assists in departmental ordering. Maintains departmental chemical inventory.

Research Scientist I: B.A./B.S. technical, minimum 3 years research and/or field application experience (water treatment experience preferred), verbal communication, and report writing skills. Conducts research in his/her area, requiring superior laboratory skills and trained powers of observation. Develops, operates, and maintains required equipment. Observes, records, interprets, and reports results of research assigned, suggests future work. Develops product formulations. Participates in field evaluations of experimental technology. Maintains technical expertise in area of responsibility.

Service Representative: College education with 15 hours of chemistry. Provides a high level of technical service to selected customers within a determined geographical area. Collects water samples at customer sites and analyzes samples. Depending on the results of the analysis, makes recommendations to adjust a variety of variables to include, but not limited to; pumps, feed rates, pressure, temperature, point of feed, etc. Develops high standards of technical knowledge and understanding of [company's] products and services through constant use and study of all company product manuals and selling tools.

WHERE WILL THE BEST JOBS BE?

There is only one sure answer to the question of who will be best prepared for the job openings that will be available in the future. The answer: Those will be best prepared who can predict most accurately where the demand will be and plan accordingly. There is more here than a cop out. There is the advice to keep one's mind on what is happening in our society that will create increased demands for what chemists do and produce. This still calls for guesswork, but it at least can focus our attention.

Let's begin with the things that determine most directly the quality of life not only here in the United States, but throughout the entire world. This brings to mind such problems as maintaining clean air, drinkable water, surroundings that lift our spirits rather than cause us to be depressed, as well as adequate supplies of energy, comfortable and afford-able housing, the wherewithal to maintain good health and physical fitness, an adequate supply of nutritious food, and everything else we find ourselves relying on from day to day.

There is no way to escape the fact that chemistry must play a key role in finding better solutions to all of these problems. How well that role is carried out will depend not only on how well our chemists are trained, but on how will-ing they are to accept the challenge of creating the products that make possible the solutions to society's problems. And this brings us to who chemists are and what they do.

Where to Look

Where to look for a chemistry-related job depends upon how far one has advanced in training and experience. People with a high school diploma usually prefer jobs that are near their homes. Fortunately, there are chemistry-related jobs in almost every community. They may include duties and responsibilities less exciting than regular chemistry, but valuable experience can be gained while working in almost any job in such facilities as water treatment, hospital laboratory testing, swimming pool maintenance, or food preparation. Obviously, chemistry-related industries offer employment opportunities for local residents.

Graduates from two-year colleges or training programs are usually less geographically limited. They can take geography into account, but it is to be expected that they will want jobs that depend more upon being trained as a chemist. This means, of course, they will have to go where the job opportunities are.

College graduates who have majored in chemistry and those who earn advanced degrees in chemistry are pretty much free to choose where they will look for employment. Beginning with becoming chemistry teachers or seeking increasingly responsible positions as practicing chemists in their home communities, they have the option of continuing the lifestyle to which they are accustomed. At the same time, they can set their sights on employment in any of the nation's most widely recognized chemical industries, private or governmental research centers, or they can combine research and teaching in universities.

BUT THERE CAN BE PROBLEMS

How difficult it will be to obtain chemistry-related jobs at any level depends upon circumstances that go beyond being trained as a chemist. When general economic conditions are on the down trend, there is sure to be stiff competition for jobs. But this will be true in all areas of employment, and it is reassuring to know that through good times and bad, more than a million people earn their living by being chemists.

Demand for new employees can change with changing economic conditions, but only in isolated situations does the number of unemployed chemists exceed the general level of unemployment.

The best insurance is to choose the field of specialization that is most likely to be needed in the industries that do well even when economic conditions are worsening. Yes, this is like advising someone to take a pill before a headache begins—but not totally so. There is at least the chance that one can think through the things that seem to affect the demand for chemists and identify those that are gaining rather than losing in importance; then act accordingly.

GETTING THAT FIRST JOB

Let's begin with the high school graduate who, for one reason or another, chooses to find a chemistry-related job before pursuing further education. Well before knocking on a potential employer's door or filling out an application form, it is a good idea to find out as much as possible about any and all agencies and industries in the community that hire chemists. Ask among friends and relatives if they know any chemists or anyone who works where chemists are employed. What you really want to know are such things as: What are the specific titles of entry-level jobs that might be available? What are the qualifications needed by people in these jobs? Who usually screens applicants?

The next step is to prepare an application letter to be either mailed or hand-carried, when it is convenient to do so. Here is an example of such a letter:

Your name
Your address
Phone number(s)

Date

Name and address of potential employer

Dear Mr./Ms._____:

Ms. Jane Smith, who is one of your employees, suggested that I apply for an entry-level job as a lab technician at (employer's organization). I will graduate from (local high school) on (date) and will come for an interview at your convenience.

I have received above average grades in chemistry, physics, and math through advanced algebra. My computer skills include the use of spreadsheets, graphic functions, file management, and word processing.

During my senior year while serving as an unpaid lab assistant, my teacher complimented me on being able to prepare solutions of specified molarity, normality, and molality, to maintain apparatus and to clean glassware. I also helped other students with such skills as titration, calorimetry, and electrochemical and preparation procedures. This work taught me the advantages of being able to write good lab reports and to label everything legibly.

I expect to enroll at the nearby junior college and, when finances permit, to try for a college degree with a major in chemistry.

Very truly yours,

(Your name)

INTERVIEWS WITH RECRUITERS

Many colleges and universities invite industrial and governmental recruiters to conduct on-campus interviews with potential employees. These interviews usually boil down to opportunities for employers to "sell" their organizations and the people being interviewed to "sell" themselves. From this point of view, the interview becomes a kind of game, albeit a very serious one in so far as the person being interviewed is concerned. In general, it is best to let the employer's representative take the lead in presenting the positive features of his or her organization. This enables the applicant to find out what kinds of people are most likely to be hired and what things count in determining their desirability. In fact, "what counts," is a key phrase used by recruiters. Time spent emphasizing one's capabilities and credentials is time wasted if it doesn't meet this "what counts" criterion.

THE INTERVIEW

The first interview is so important that it pays to practice the role of job applicant with some one with whom you feel at ease and who will help you make a good first impression. And there is always the good advice to be well groomed, on time, and courteous. Be ready to answer questions but don't be too anxious to hawk your capabilities. It is usually best to assume that the potential employer treats employees fairly and pays the going wages. One can always ask later for a raise or for improvements in working conditions.

These suggestions make good sense for people who wait until they complete college level courses in chemistry before seeking employment. At this level, competition for jobs increases, and applicants may have to go where jobs are available. Chemistry faculty members usually keep in touch with where there are employment opportunities. Asking for their advice gives them a stake in your chances of finding the job you want.

Firm offers of employment are seldom made until a representative or executives of the employing organization have visited with the applicant. These visits may be arranged on campus or in the home town of the applicant, but many organizations extend invitations to serious applicants to come to the organization's location at their expense. The employer wants to evaluate your professional and personal attributes firsthand, and it is equally important that you like the prospective employer and want to move into the community.

In general, employers expect applicants to ask questions, but common sense says that the applicant should use tact and diplomacy, especially during the getting-acquainted phase of an interview. You should learn where positions are available, the products or services with which you will be working, and the nature, duties, and scope of specific openings for which you are being considered. If a specific opening is identified, find out whether it is a new position, if it is permanent or temporary, whether it is dependent upon a government or other short-term contract. Ask about training periods and the kind of supervision you will have.

SENSITIVE QUESTIONS

If the interview is going well, you may ask about the organization's promotion and transfer policies, working hours and facilities, moving expense policies, safety facilities, policies involving publications and attendance at professional meetings. As the interview unfolds, you usually can estimate how enthusiastic the employer is becoming about your capabilities and personal attributes. If indications are that you will have the decision to face to accept or reject a job offer, you can afford to ask increasingly significant questions. But you should use tact. You can ask about the history of the employing organization, its expansion rate, and expectations for the future. Other questions can help you learn more about the type of organization. Questions regarding salary are especially sensitive. It is not that the question should not be asked so much as the timing. Most employers have found that salary alone does not determine an employer's impression on an applicant, and many applicants soon learn that salary alone does not determine the desirability of a job. So it is wise to allow the salary question to fit nicely into the total interview.

MAKING OTHER CONTACTS

The placement offices that are maintained by colleges and universities provide valuable services. Many potential employers prefer to work through these agencies, and placement officers take pride in seeing the people they represent obtain the best possible jobs. It is important that the necessary registration forms be completed early in such a way that will impress favorably potential employers.

Scientific and professional organizations, particularly the American Chemical Society (ACS) in the United States and The Chemical Institute of Canada (CIC), devote a good share of their interests to helping new chemists find jobs and experienced chemists advance in their profession. Chemistry departments at both the high school and collegiate levels are encouraged to request a list of the publications that describe the services that are provided by these organizations. The wide variety of materials includes booklets, posters, and videotapes to serve all educational levels. Sample titles include,

"What a Chemist Should Consider Before Accepting a Government Position," "Planning for Graduate Work in Chemistry," "A Career as a Chemical Technician," and "I Know You're a Chemist, But What Do You Do?" Examples of professional development services that are offered for members and student affiliates include: a computerized list of potential employers and the names and credentials of chemists who are seeking jobs, a national employment clearinghouse at national and regional meetings where job seekers can interview potential employers, a career consulting program whereby members can gain advice by phone on job search strategies, interview techniques, and resume preparation.

Valuable information and services are also provided by the American Institute of Chemists at 7315 Wisconsin Avenue, Bethesda, MD 20814, and the American Institute of Chemical Engineers at 345 East 47th Street, New York, NY 10017.

APPLICATION LETTERS AND RESUMES

It is to be expected that job applicants prepare a well-crafted letter to earn an interview with a potential employer. And today, the design and presentation of the resume has become a test of one's ability to make maximum use of devices and formats that attract attention and convey the impression that the author is, in general, up to date.

With this in mind, we cite "Tips on Resume Preparation," a highly informative booklet available at no cost from the American Chemical Society. Included are examples of resumes that are designed to accommodate a range of job applications, the curriculum vitae, and the covering letter. These examples become efficient guidelines for presenting one's personal qualities, hopes, and ambitions, something that is often as important as the facts of one's training and experience.

CHAPTER 8

SOME FACTS AND FIGURES

FIRST, CHEMISTRY IS WORLDWIDE

Chemistry is the men and women who teach chemistry in high schools, colleges, and universities throughout the world. They keep the profession and industry of chemistry alive. Especially at the university level, these men and women team up with research people in industrial and governmental laboratories to discover new or better ways to keep us all well fed, clothed, comfortable, healthy, and in touch with each other and with the natural world.

In the United States, chemistry is the 340,000 women and 720,000 men whose jobs depend upon the chemical industry. Half of these people are employed in production and the others are in various supporting roles. The chemical industry also supports 90,000 scientists and engineers.

Chemistry is the lab technicians in our hospitals and health clinics who tell physicians and surgeons whether dozens of our body's chemistries are doing what they should be doing. Chemistry is also their counterparts in local and national agencies who tell us the water we drink is safe and the food we eat is nutritious and uncontaminated.

Chemistry is the men and women who do the chores that come with producing, packaging, and distributing the hundreds of products of the chemical industry, and the research people who seek better ways to turn out these products and to improve those that are already on the market.

From other points of view, chemistry is approximately 9,000 men and women who earn bachelor's degrees in chemistry each year, 1,700 who earn master's degrees, and 2,200 who qualify for the doctorate. And for those who major in chemical engineering, 4,400 receive bachelor's degrees, 800 master's, and 550 earn the doctorate. And these numbers apply to the United States only. In all but the most underdeveloped nations, people look upon advanced training in chemistry as a way to make the most possible of what they have going for them.

Chemistry is the 146,000 members of the American Chemical Society with their $220 million annual budget to be spent for the advancement of the profession and industry. And the 5,000 members of the American Federation of Chemists with their $500,000 annual budget. And the 180-member Chemical Manufacturers Association with their $5 million annual budget to be spent for the advancement of the chemical industry. And the 57,000 members of the American Institute of Chemical Engineers with their $5 million annual budget. Here, again, there are comparable organizations in many other nations.

From yet another point of view, chemistry provides the paycheck for thousands of secretaries, lawyers, accountants, custodians, and other people who may benefit only indirectly by knowing something of the ways and means of chemistry.

SECOND, CHEMISTRY IS A WAY
TO MAKE A LIVING

Entry-level jobs in the United States that require no training beyond high school chemistry may pay little more than the minimum wage. Add a year or two of chemistry courses beyond the high school level, and the average wage doubles or even triples. Add a bachelor's degree, and the starting salary moves up to an average of $27,500. For those who hold a master's degree, the average starting salary (1995) is $39,000, and for Ph.D.'s $59,000. For chemical engineers, comparable figures are: $39,000, $44,000, and $57,000. With experience comes salary increases, especially for chemists and chemical engineers below the doctorate level.

THIRD, CHEMISTRY IS PRODUCTS

Fundamentally, nearly everything that is to be found in supermarkets, shopping malls, drug stores, automobile showrooms, and all manner of sales outlets becomes available by taking apart some kinds of molecules and putting the fragments together in new combinations. The only exceptions are the things we use that consist of only one kind of atom, for example, silver, gold, mercury, oxygen, helium, or one of nature's other ninety or so elements.

There is an enormously wide range in the quantities of the products that chemists produce. For sulfuric acid, the substance of greatest demand in the United States, each person's share is measured in hundreds of pounds. At the same time, the total production of a new medicine is measured in micrograms. And costs can range from pennies per pound to hundreds of times the equivalent weight in gold.

Chemistry is also world trade. Nearly all nations both import and export products from the chemical industry. Canada, the United Kingdom, and Germany, for example, import on the average $400 worth of chemicals for each citizen; the United States approximately one-third this amount. At the same time there is a wide variation in the per capita amount of chemicals exported by these nations. These amounts are: Canada, $250; United Kingdom, $500; Germany, $700; United States, $200.

FOURTH, CHEMISTRY IS PROCESS

Chemistry is one of humanity's best ways of understanding how things happen. At times teaming up with physics, chemists describe nature's events and circumstances as they occur at the level of atoms and molecules. In doing so, they free humanity from fearing and being at the mercy of the physical environment. On the contrary, fear is replaced by appreciation and the ability to manage, conserve, and improve the utilization of our natural resources.

And if we move toward the leading edge of the chemical enterprise, chemists are teaming up with people in all branches of science to better understand why people behave as they do and how best to take full advantage of what it means to be alive. The point being made here is that there are no limits to where careers in chemistry can lead. As we have tried to show in the earlier chapters in this book, chemistry opens the door to the realization of all kinds of hopes and ambitions.

CHAPTER 9

PROFESSIONAL ASSOCIATIONS AND SOCIETIES

Chemical societies, institutes, and other professional organizations play important roles not only in advancing the interests of their members but also in improving the public's image of who chemists are and what they do. Although their statements of what they stand for are reviewed periodically, the current wordings represent points of view that promise to continue far into the future.

THE CODE OF ETHICS OF THE CHEMICAL INSTITUTE OF CANADA

As professional chemists, chemical engineers, or technologists, the members of The Chemical Institute of Canada and its Constituent Societies adhere to the following ethical premises:

(a), to dedicate themselves to high ideals of personal honour and professional integrity.

(b), to accept and defend the paramountcy of public well-being. In observance of these premises, they promote the following actions:

(1), to practice their professions to the best of their ability;

(2), to encourage others to observe high professional standards;

(3), to act responsibly in discharging obligations to the public and to employers;

(4), to sign and to seal only documents that have been prepared by them under their direct supervision;

(5), to accept financial compensation only for professional services rendered; and

(6), to promote an understanding of the social consequences of advances in chemical science, engineering and technology.

THE AMERICAN INSTITUTE OF CHEMISTS CODE OF ETHICS

It is the duty of the chemist:

(1) To uphold the law; not to engage in illegal work nor cooperate with anyone so engaged;

(2) To avoid associating or being identified with any enterprise of questionable character;

(3) To be diligent in exposing and opposing such errors and frauds as the chemist's special knowledge brings to light;

(4) To sustain the institutions and burdens of the community as a responsible citizen;

(5) To work and act in a strict spirit of fairness to employers, clients, contractors, and employees, and in a spirit of personal helpfulness and fraternity toward other members of the chemical profession;

(6) To use only honorable means of competition for professional employment; to advertise only in a dignified and factual manner; to refrain from unfairly injuring, directly or indirectly, the professional reputation, prospects, or business of a fellow chemist, or attempting to supplant a fellow chemist already selected for employment; to perform services for a client only at rates that fairly reflect costs of equipment, supplies, and overhead expenses as well as fair personal compensation;

(7) To accept employment from more than one employer or client only when there is no conflict of interest; to accept commissions or compensation in any form from more than one interested party only with the full knowledge and consent of all parties concerned;

(8) To perform all professional work in a manner that merits full confidence and trust; to be conservative in estimates, reports, and testimony, especially if these are related to the promotion of a business enterprise or the protection of the public interest, and to state explicitly any known bias embodied therein; to advise client or employer of the probability of success before undertaking a project;

(9) To review the professional work of other chemists, when requested, fairly and in confidence, whether they are (a) subordinates or employees, (b) authors of proposals for grants or contracts, (c) authors of technical papers, patents, or other publications, or (d) involved in litigation;

(10) To advance the profession by exchanging general information and experience with fellow chemists and by contributing to the work of technical societies and to the technical press when such contribution does not conflict with the interests of a client or employer;

to announce inventions and scientific advances first in this way rather than through the public press; to ensure that credit for technical work is given to its actual authors;

(11) To work for any client or employer under a clear agreement, preferably in writing, as to the ownership of data, plans, improvements, inventions, designs, or other intellectual property developed or discovered while so employed, understanding that in the absence of a written agreement:

   (a) results based on information from the client or employer, not obtainable elsewhere, are the property of the client or employer,

   (b) results based on knowledge or information belonging to the chemist, or publicly available, are the property of the chemist, the client or employer being entitled to their use only in the case or project for which the chemist was retained,

   (c) all work and results outside of the field for which the chemist was retained or employed, and not using time or facilities belonging to a client or employer, are the property of the chemist, and

   (d) special data or information provided by a client or employer, or created by the chemist and belonging to the client or employer, must be treated as confidential, used only in general as a part of the chemist's professional experience, and published only after release by the client or employer;

(12) To report any infractions of these principles of professional conduct to the authorities responsible for enforcement of applicable laws or regulations, or to

the Ethics Committee of The American Institute of Chemists, as appropriate.

Approved by Board of Directors, April 29, 1983.

THE OBJECTIVES OF THE
AMERICAN CHEMICAL SOCIETY

The largest professional organization of chemists, the American Chemical Society, states its objectives to be:

1. to encourage in the broadest and most liberal manner the advancement of chemistry in all its branches
2. the promotion of research in chemical science and industry
3. the improvement of the qualifications and usefulness of chemists through high standards of professional ethics, education, and attainments
4. the increase and diffusion of chemical knowledge; and
5. by its meetings, professional contacts, reports, papers, discussions, and publications, to promote scientific interests and inquiry.
   Thereby
   a. fostering public welfare and education
   b. aiding the development of the country's industries, and
   c. adding to the material prosperity and happiness of our people.

Actually, the professional organizations of chemistry are fundamentally the voices and votes of their members. In other words, chemists govern themselves as a profession.

All qualified chemists are encouraged to join their societies, institutes, and associations and take active roles in conducting business and advancing programs. Many organizations carry out their programs through various committees. These committees provide many opportunities for individual members to lend a hand and voice. For example, the standing committees of the Board of Directors of the American Chemical Society include: Awards and Recognitions; Chemical Abstracts Service; Education and Students; Finance; Grants and Fellowships; Public, Professional, and Member Relations; and Publications.

Through extensive programs of national, regional, and local meetings, their organizations provide many opportunities for chemists to exchange information, compare viewpoints, and to let the public know what the chemical profession is up to. At local meetings, chemists in the same geographical area can get acquainted with each other in addition to pooling ideas and points of view. At national meetings, with thousands of chemists attending, each member is almost sure to find other people who are interested in and can help advance research on his or her favorite project.

Through many publications, the professional organizations help their members keep pace with the many new developments in the science and technology of chemistry. An outstanding example is the *Chemical Abstracts* service of the American Chemical Society. Through this service, all articles on chemistry and chemical engineering published anywhere in the world, as fast as they can be found by extensive and far-flung searching, are abstracted and indexed by experts. All modern data retrieval methods are used to make these abstracts available to the total scientific fraternity.

CHAPTER 10

CHEMISTRY YESTERDAY, TODAY, AND TOMORROW

There are things about chemistry that do not change. Its basic purpose is to produce materials and to help us better understand, appreciate, and manage nature's chemistry. This has always been and always will be. What does change are the answers to the what, how, and why of chemistry. And it is these changes that are of special concern for people who are contemplating careers in chemistry.

Chemistry has long played a role in people's affairs, from the most primitive to the most modern. One feature of this role in early societies is illustrated when Shakespeare has Macbeth needing something to serve as a security blanket, life-support system, and all-around bodyguard. Among the twenty or so of the raw materials needed to cook up the required product were: "Eye of newt, and toe of frog/Wool of bat, and tongue of dog/Adder's fork, and blind-worm's sting/Lizard's leg, and howlet's wing."

FROM SHAKESPEARE TO THE NATIONAL INSTITUTES OF HEALTH

It is the "toe of frog" in the witches brew that comes to mind when we consider the work of a modern-day chemist,

Dr. John Daly. Frogs provide the raw materials for his research, but the why and how of his work has come a long, long way from, "Double, double toil and trouble;/Fire burn; and cauldron bubble."

It was known even before Shakespeare's time that frogs produce substances that can have intense effects on life processes. Indians in Columbia, for example, have a long history of using a substance from the skin of native frogs that is amazingly toxic. The darts for their blowguns, when dipped in this substance, administer a lethal dose to animals being hunted for food.

Amazonian Indians provide an even more exotic example. They use an excretion from a local species of frogs as the active ingredient in an almost magic potion. They collect mucus secretions from the frog's skin on flat, little sticks that are then kiln dried and stored for later use. When it is time to go hunting, the hunters burn themselves slightly with live coals, moisten the sticks with saliva, and then rub the preparation into the burned areas. After surviving a day or so of intense sickness, they believe their hunting abilities will now be greatly enhanced. They now have the courage that is needed to seek game in dangerous places.

Dr. Daly and his research team at the National Institutes of Health have spent more than thirty years isolating and identifying the properties of substances produced by frogs, particularly several brightly colored species that are native to Central America, Columbia, and Ecuador. He has also obtained useful substances from frogs native to Brazil, Argentina, Uruguay, Madagascar, Australia, Africa, and Thailand. In addition to his own research, he has helped other scientists to better understand where frogs fit into nature's grand scheme of things, including discovering nearly a dozen new species.

Some 300 different kinds of molecules have been isolated from the tissues and secretions of frogs. Some were totally new discoveries, and nearly all have been found to have properties that are of much interest. Many are toxic, some amazingly so. One substance, adenoregulin, that was isolated from the hunting potion, for example, has remarkable effects on brain functions and, consequently, on how people behave.

Another substance, epibatidine, recently has been isolated from the tissues of a brightly colored frog native to the Pacific highlands in Ecuador. This new discovery has remarkable pain relieving properties, 200 times more potent than morphine, in some cases. Epibatidine affects the nervous system in very much the same way as does nicotine; but much more intensely. Research people who are working on the drug addiction phenomenon are interested in epibatidine because the more pronounced the effect, the more easily the cause can be determined.

From the point of view of better appreciating the why of chemistry, it is significant to note that no specific need initiated the research that led to the discovery of epibatidine and its amazing properties. Once the new substance was discovered, however, the logical next step was to see if these properties could fulfill a need, a state of affairs that seems to be in keeping with the kinds of motivation that bring people to careers in chemistry.

A GLIMPSE OF TOMORROW'S CHEMISTRY

A rapidly developing field of research promises to merge with and add a new dimension to the kind of work Dr. Daly has been doing. Frogs are not alone in producing molecules that make life's processes what they are. The same can be said of all of life's myriad forms. And no matter how fantastically complex these molecules or how wonderful their properties, they are all the result of taking apart the molecules of raw materials and reassembling the fragments to form new combinations.

This is the domain of DNA. Today's chemists are completing giant steps toward identifying the specific gene or genes that "code for" the production of many kinds of molecules—even molecules that are too complex to be assembled by the most advanced synthesizing procedures. Furthermore, once the gene that custom designs a specific molecule has been identified in one life form, it can be reproduced and introduced into the genome of a substitute organism, which lends itself to becoming a commercial source of the original molecule.

The availability of adequate quantities of newly discovered substances that affect life's processes can create new opportunities to solve difficult problems. There are also problems, however, in taking advantage of these opportunities. The term *biopsychosocial,* as used earlier to describe drug addiction, illustrates these kinds of problems and what they will mean to tomorrow's chemists. The *bio* part of the term refers to the whole new world of molecules whose production is controlled by genes. The *psych* part refers to the brain where one's needs, interests, and behavior are controlled. The *socio* part takes into account the fact that the needs and interests of any one person are sure to affect and be affected by the needs and interests of others.

CHEMISTS CAN EXPECT CONTROVERSY

Chemists are expected to produce materials that promise to fulfill everyone's needs, but sometimes fulfilling the needs of one group occurs at the expense of other people's needs and interests. And this can be both good and bad. It is good that chemists can have a voice in determining the kinds of problems they believe are worthy of their efforts to solve. But there is trouble ahead when the public image of chemists makes it difficult for them to gain the respect and cooperation of those who must provide the "psych" and "socio" expertise that is essential if society's problems are to be solved. All of which is to say that careers in chemistry offer open-ended opportunities to join forces with people in other professions in making one's life count for something that will be really worthwhile.

HISTORY REVISITED

It would be misleading to leave the impression that chemistry began with such activities as witches cooking up magic potions. Chemistry began when people first wanted to know why one substance served some purpose better than another, or why certain substances would relieve aches and pains, hunger or discomfort. Chemistry developed in the things people need to do every day—cooking, baking, brewing, building, working with metals, mining, washing, dying, art, medicine, and on and on.

Even though early chemists spent their time doing such everyday things as making soaps or dyes, winning metals from their ores, or distilling elixirs from herbs, for one reason or other, their neighbors were inclined to associate what they were doing with witchcraft and primitive medicine men. Early chemists risked being looked upon with suspicion lest they were in partnership with the devil or other evil spirits. Not always did those chemists, or alchemists as they were known then, hire public relations experts to improve their image. On the contrary, they were more inclined to use the flames and smoke, unexpected explosions, or color changes of their public demonstrations to enhance the notion that they knew things and could do things that were not available to ordinary people.

THE IMAGE OF CHEMISTRY
BACK A LONG WAY

Looking back to the time Columbus was discovering America, the public's notion of who chemists are and what they contribute to a society's well-being was pretty much overshadowed by the widely publicized efforts of a few alchemists who dreamed of accomplishing amazing things, like cooking up the "philosopher's stone" and using its miraculous ability to change base metals into gold or ensure its owner perfect health, happiness, or whatever he or she wanted. It is to be expected that anyone who promised to achieve such a grandiose product would be held in awe by everyone—kings, princes, popes, and commoners.

At the same time, there was a flourishing market for the products that the chemists of the day could actually produce. These chemists, in effect, allowed the alchemists to go about their business while they spent their time producing the materials that were needed to keep civilization advancing. There is irony in how the alchemists, with their exaggerated promises, were able to mess up the image of chemistry while much progress was being made in producing dyes and pigments, glass and earthenware, and alloys and other materials whose properties measure up well when compared with the efforts of the best of today's chemists.

Until the early 1800s chemistry consisted of little more than a collection of formulas and recipes for extracting desired substances from their natural sources or blending raw materials into the desired products. Only a few people had tried to create theories or general principles to account for the things they observed when bringing off their reactions. So long as the recipe turned out the desired product, there seemed to be only slight tendencies to question the why and wherefore of the whole process. Nor was much chemical knowledge published. Successful methods and recipes were jealously guarded and usually passed along from friend to friend or from parents to children. Rulers who were fortunate enough to have a deposit of some rare but useful raw material in their territories resorted to war, if necessary, to protect their good fortune.

FROM RECIPES TO MENTAL MODELS

Early in the 1800s the investigations of several chemists in England and on the continent of Europe began to point more and more to the idea that all matter is composed of fantastically tiny particles, and that chemical reactions are actually limited to rearrangements rather than the breaking up of these particles.

Further research suggested that there are only a few different kinds of these particles, in contrast to countless substances that can be put together by combining different kinds and numbers of the tiny particles. It was this idea that all chemistry is built around the rearranging or reshuffling of a reasonably small number of different kinds of atoms that did more than anything else to unify chemistry—to bring order out of a chaotic collection of formulas and recipes.

With the development of the atomic theory of the composition of all matter, the chemists of the day began to divide into two categories. Craftspeople continued to follow their formulas and recipes and turn out the desired products.

Chemists, who were more inclined to ask how and why, devoted more and more of their capabilities to clarifying the newly devised scheme of atoms and the atomic theory. The infinitely small size of these particles and the equally large numbers present in the tiniest visible sample of anything forced the men and women who worked with atomic theory to operate almost entirely at an abstract, mental-model level.

Throughout much of the nineteenth century, thousands of chemists devoted their lifetimes to "the occurrence, preparation, properties, and uses of" one or another element or compound. Thousands of separate reactions were carried out and described with as much precision as the day's measuring instruments permitted. A much smaller number of chemists, with a more theoretical bent, looked for orderly relationships among the observations of these separate reactions—observations that would support the orderly relationships they wanted to weave into the atomic theory.

It was not that the atomic theory (as conceived by John Dalton early in the 1800s) wouldn't support the chemical industry of the nineteenth century. It did. Chemists were able to write the recipes for new reactions and predict yields with good precision. Nor was the prediction of the properties of newly synthesized substances purely guesswork. The combining capacities of the atoms of the earth's elements were well known. But many questions continued to bother chemists.

Near the close of the nineteenth century, several isolated fields of investigation began producing observations that called for reconsidering several of the firmly established ideas about atoms, especially their total indestructibility. In the minds of several investigators, the hard, indestructible atoms as conceived by John Dalton were beginning to come apart. If atoms were totally indestructible, William Roentgen, for example, couldn't explain why the photographic film left near one of his new X-ray machines blackened, even though it was still in its light-proof wrapping. Nor could Henry Becquerel explain the similar blackening of film left too close to selected mineral specimens from his rock collection. But it was the work of the Curies that demanded most directly that the idea of the indestructibility of atoms needed to be reconsidered. Their observations of the natural radioactivity of certain minerals, especially pitchblende, not only led them to the discovery of new elements (polonium and radium) but also to the realization that radioactive atoms eject tiny fragments of themselves at the moment of exhibiting their radioactivity.

Precise description of these atomic fragments became the goal of twentieth-century scientists all over the world. Before the century reached the halfway mark, the properties of electrons, protons, neutrons, and other subatomic particles were well known. Furthermore, the way these particles are packed together to form each of the ninety or so different kinds of atoms in the known elements had been described with sufficient precision to allow physicists and chemists to release and control the enormous quantities of energy involved in atomic fission and fusion. From the chemist's point of view, the structure of each element's atoms was clarified sufficiently to provide a theoretical basis for explaining or predicting the chemical behavior of each element—particularly the behavior involved in the kinds and number of bonds one atom can form with another.

With ever-increasing knowledge of the structure of atoms has come increasing challenge to manipulate the "architecture" of molecules and thus put together new molecules with predictable properties—or to whittle away from already available molecules the portion that gives them undesirable properties.

It is difficult to imagine anything happening that would seriously diminish the number of long-term opportunities for chemists to obtain jobs. But it is a gamble to predict which fields of chemistry-related jobs and careers are most likely to create the most opportunities in the future. The success of such predictions stands to be influenced by anticipating which problems in our society deserve or demand the most attention.

WHERE WILL FUTURE MARKETS BE?

It may be, for example, that the chemistry of plastics, textiles, paints and varnishes, and similar materials for fabricating buildings and furnishings will advance to the point where potential customers are totally satisfied with what is currently available. But they might be less content with currently available drugs and medicines. Under these circumstances, the number of job opportunities in pharmaceutical chemistry would increase while those in the plastic industry would decrease. Similarly, it might be that the chemistry of dyes and detergents becomes more advanced than, say, the chemistry of rubber or glass. This prediction would advise people who are looking ahead to chemistry-related employment to pay special attention to the concepts and principles that are particularly involved in the chemistry of rubber or glass.

The strategy here is to judge the up-to-dateness of the chemistry that makes possible the materials or commodities that are essential to a specific commercial product. But this does not take into account how the public's wants and needs can change. We might determine that the chemistry of cosmetics lags behind other areas of applied chemistry. But it could be that ten years or so into the future, styles and fashions could move abruptly toward a completely "natural" look. And job opportunities in the cosmetic industry would decrease.

Another kind of strategy looks at current solutions to major societal problems to see if the available supply of essential raw materials might become inadequate. In the early 1970s, for example, the United States experienced a shortage of petroleum, a totally essential fuel and the raw material for thousands of manufactured products. Although the shortage seems to have been more contrived than actual, many chemists were needed to adjust production processes and to conduct research that would be essential were we forced to adjust to a petroleum deficient economy.

There is more. The urgency with which our society chooses to look for solutions to some rather than other problems can influence where job opportunities increase or decrease. Predicting these choices calls for a full measure of gambler's courage. In many cases economic, political, even philosophical interests are put at risk. Widely recognized examples are the continued fouling of the environment, the conservation of fossil fuel resources, population control, and providing adequate food and housing for everyone.

FOCUSING ON ENVIRONMENTAL PROBLEMS

Using environmental problems as a specific example, opportunities for chemists would certainly increase if the public were to really rebel against having to breathe an atmosphere made painfully noxious by exhaust from improperly maintained automobiles, trucks, buses, planes, public and private incinerators, and smokestacks. Everyone's personal freedom and purses are involved when we consider the nation's waterways, from the largest rivers to the smallest creeks; not to mention our lakes and oceans. And the sources of these problems are equally widespread. They can begin with eroding farmlands or housing developments bulldozed clean of all water-storing vegetation. Less visible but posing ever increasingly serious problems are all of the wastes that we supposedly get rid of by dumping them down sewers: human waste, animal remains, swill, and a rich mixture of domestic, municipal, and industrial garbage.

On the good news side, the current generation of chemists working with other scientists have proved that it is possible to improve air and water quality at selected locations. This adds reality to the challenge that everyone can enjoy a pollution free environment—a challenge that would require the dedicated efforts of many chemists. The chemistry of any environment is very complex. To get at the true causes of a single city's smog-filled air or polluted river requires a wealth of information that is hard to come by. What is in the air or water, who is putting it there, and how pollutants are interacting with nature's ways of cleaning the environment must be determined. The interdependence among all forms of life adds another degree of complexity to all environmental pollution problems.

Three examples flesh out what is being said here. Late in the 1900s it was observed that the amount of ultraviolet radiation reaching the earth was becoming greater and thereby increasing the incidence of skin cancers and eye cataracts, not to mention the possible harmful effects on the total biosphere. Chemists traced the origins of this problem to certain gases being discharged into the atmosphere, particularly, chloroflurocarbons (CFCs) and methane. It was known that a layer of ozone above the atmosphere shielded the earth from excessive ultraviolet radiation. Research proved that these ozone molecules, when impacted by photons from the sun, could initiate a multistep reaction that converted the ozone to oxygen. And oxygen is much less opaque to ultraviolet radiation.

One obvious solution to the ozone depletion problem is to decrease the amount of CFCs and methane being discharged into the atmosphere. The trouble with this solution is that it is easier said than done. CFCs are the refrigerant of choice in air conditioners and refrigerators and as the propellant in spray cans. And methane escapes into the atmosphere from sources as widespread as poorly maintained gas wells and the digestive tracts of cattle.

The chemistry profession and industry has already made much progress in developing substitute materials that do what CFCs do but do not pose a threat to the ozone layer. We will continue to enjoy the benefits of air-conditioning and the convenience of aerosol sprays. But this doesn't necessarily mean that there will no longer be a demand for chemists who have the credentials that enable them to deal with the ozone and related upper-atmosphere problems.

A somewhat similar problem began with the recognition of an increase in the acidity of rain falling in areas where certain kinds of polluting gases were being discharged into the atmosphere. With the increasing acidity of the precipitation, there was an increase in such actions as the corrosion of metals; the erosion of marble, limestone, and other carbonate building materials and statuary; and interference with the normal metabolism of many aquatic life forms.

Alleviation of the acid-rain problem was accomplished by tracing its origin to the discharge of sulfur and nitrogen oxides into the atmosphere. Scrubbers installed at the sources of these gases, together with converting to less polluting fuels, has pretty much solved this environmental pollution problem.

A third environmental problem can be traced to the effects of the sun's rays on the temperature of the earth. Some kinds of gases, if present in the atmosphere, allow sunlight to pass through, but the longer wavelengths are converted into heat. It has been observed that greater concentrations of carbon dioxide, methane, CFCs, and nitrogen oxides increase the heat trapping ability of the atmosphere. This results in global warming, commonly called the greenhouse effect. The ultimate effects and possible solutions of this problem promise to add indefinitely to the number of job opportunities for chemists.

Environmental pollution problems pose special problems. Their solutions invariably turn out to be very expensive, and corrective measures often interfere with personal or corporate business enterprises. This leads to disagreements about who is responsible and the degree to which the public's interests are at risk. Chemists risk being caught in the middle of these disagreements. At times their judgment as to causes and consequences is at stake. And they stand to be blamed for the cost and consequences of actions that were based on their analyses of specific situations.

At the same time, there are satisfactions in being able to share technical knowledge and know-how with the public rather than to shy away from civic responsibilities. If the complex circumstances that determine the condition of the environment not only locally but worldwide are to be effectively managed, it may well be up to chemists to organize all of the economic and political interests whose decisions either support or stand in the way of corrective actions.

KEEPING HUMANITY WELL FED

Chemists hold a key position in keeping people well fed. Here, too, they must serve the interests of producers, processors, distributors, and consumers. At the production level, it is up to chemistry to find ways to keep livestock healthy, to ensure maximum yields from farm crops and orchards, and to keep negative side effects to a minimum.

New processing and distributing practices require improved packaging materials. Along with protecting the contents from dirt and moisture, there is always the possibility that a newly developed product might react badly with old or new packaging materials. Increasing demand for gourmet or exotic dishes, coupled with the tendency to want to spend less time in one's own kitchen, confronts chemists with the challenge to produce a package that will accept almost any concoction, hold it indefinitely in frozen food cases or on supermarket shelves, and deliver it to the family table in good condition.

Part of the role chemists play in keeping us well fed comes to mind when we read the list of ingredients in representative foods. The label on a loaf of specialty bread, for example, lists a dozen or more ingredients none of which appears in an ordinary recipe for baking bread. These additives are included because someone has found a need to improve the bread's nutritive value, enhance its flavor, impart a desirable color, or extend shelf life. Chemists come up with the kinds of molecules that have the properties required to meet these needs. The needs are not necessarily their responsibility, but they are responsible for the efficiency and safety of how they are fulfilled.

People have long used salt to preserve meats, added spices and herbs to improve the flavor of prepared foods, preserved fruits with sugar, and pickled vegetables in vinegar. In recent years, both food producers and processors and their customers have looked for ways to increase the efficiency of food protection and preservation. This has led to legislation regulating the kinds and amounts of additives than can be used. These regulations are based on the best available estimates of how a potential additive will affect normal life processes—something that adds both opportunities and responsibilities for chemists.

Similar circumstances developed from recent legislation requiring labels to show the kinds and amounts of various nutrients and other components present in normal servings of nearly all kinds of food. Newly approved labels require determining the amount per serving of saturated fat, cholesterol, dietary fiber, sodium, and so forth. Chemists are also called on to improve the quantitative meaning of such advertising terms as "light," "low-fat," and "high-fiber." The intent here is to help consumers monitor their intake of all nutrients and avoid items that may threaten their health.

Biochemists, those who specialize in the chemistry of life's processes, are taking on new levels of responsibility where genes from one species are being introduced into the genomes of food-producing plants and animals. Each new gene that is introduced into a variety of tomatoes, for example, will change the kinds of molecules that are responsible for at least one characteristic of that variety of tomato. It may become more disease resistant, ship better, have longer shelf life, or taste better. At the same time, the newly added characteristic may cause this variety of tomato to cause an allergy in some people, even after it has been processed to make tomato paste or used to prepare pizzas.

In the United States the Food and Drug Administration employs chemists who work closely with those employed by food-producing companies that use genetic engineering to improve their products. This is a good example of how the chemistry profession and industry provides a wide range of opportunities for people who like to make their own decisions about how best to make one's life count for something.

ADDITIONAL READINGS

Atkins, P. W. *The Periodic Kingdom: A Journey into the Land of the Chemical Elements.* New York: Basic Books, 1995.

Brown, Sheldon S. *Opportunities in Biotechnology Careers.* Lincolnwood, IL: VGM Career Books, 1994.

Corrick, James A. *Recent Revolutions in Chemistry.* New York: Watts, 1986.

Easton, Thomas A. *Careers in Science.* Lincolnwood, IL: VGM Career Books, 1990.

Fanning, Odom. *Environmental Careers.* Lincolnwood, IL: VGM Career Books, 1991.

Gable, Fred B. *Careers in Pharmacy.* Lincolnwood, IL: VGM Career Books, 1990.

Gray, Harry B., John D. Simon, and William C. Trogler. *Braving the Elements.* Sausalito, CA: University Science Books, 1995. Chemistry and its total significance.

Hoffmann, Roald. *The Same and Not the Same.* New York: Columbia University Press, 1995. Nature of chemistry and its relation to other branches of science.

Karni, Karen R. and Jane Sidney Oliver. *Opportunities in Medical Technology.* Lincolnwood, IL: VGM Career Books, 1990.

Resumes for Scientific and Technical Careers. Lincolnwood, IL: VGM Career Books, 1993.

Snyder, Carl H. *The Extraordinary Chemistry of Ordinary Things.* New York: Wiley, 1995.

Woodburn, John H. *Opportunities in Energy Careers.* Lincolnwood, IL: VGM Books, 1992.

Woodburn, John H. *Taking Things Apart and Putting Things Together.* Washington, DC.: The American Chemical Society, 1976. What chemistry is, what chemists do, and the results.